Catholic Social Teaching

Catholic Social Teaching

A User's Guide

WILLIAM O'NEILL, SJ

ORBIS BOOKS
Maryknoll, New York 10545

Founded in 1970, Orbis Books endeavors to publish works that enlighten the mind, nourish the spirit, and challenge the conscience. The publishing arm of the Maryknoll Fathers and Brothers, Orbis seeks to explore the global dimensions of the Christian faith and mission, to invite dialogue with diverse cultures and religious traditions, and to serve the cause of reconciliation and peace. The books published reflect the views of their authors and do not represent the official position of the Maryknoll Society. To learn more about Orbis Books, please visit our website at www.orbisbooks.com.

Manufactured in the United States of America.

Manuscript editing and typesetting by Joan Weber Laflamme.

Library of Congress Cataloging-in-Publication Data

Names: O'Neill, William, 1927– author.

Title: Catholic social teaching : a user's guide / William O'Neill, SJ.

Description: Maryknoll, NY : Orbis Books, [2021] | Includes bibliographical references and index. | Summary: "A guide to key themes of the Catholic social teaching tradition and its implications for ethical issues such as war, peacemaking, and the global refugee crisis"— Provided by publisher.

Identifiers: LCCN 2020040741 (print) | LCCN 2020040742 (ebook) | ISBN 9781626984172 (trade paperback) | ISBN 9781608338801 (epub)

Subjects: LCSH: Catholic Church—Doctrines. | Christian sociology—Catholic Church. | Christian ethics—Catholic authors.

Classification: LCC BX1753 .O644 2021 (print) | LCC BX1753 (ebook) | DDC 261.088/282—dc23

LC record available at https://lccn.loc.gov/2020040741

LC ebook record available at https://lccn.loc.gov/2020040742

Contents

Part Two
Applications

Appendix

A Word about Intrinsic Evil   151

A Prayer for Our Earth

All-powerful God, you are present in the whole universe
and in the smallest of your creatures.
You embrace with your tenderness all that exists.
Pour out upon us the power of your love,
that we may protect life and beauty.
Fill us with peace, that we may live
as brothers and sisters, harming no one.
O God of the poor,
help us to rescue the abandoned and forgotten of this earth,
so precious in your eyes.
Bring healing to our lives,
that we may protect the world and not prey on it,
that we may sow beauty, not pollution and destruction.
Touch the hearts
of those who look only for gain
at the expense of the poor and the earth.
Teach us to discover the worth of each thing,
to be filled with awe and contemplation,
to recognize that we are profoundly united
with every creature
as we journey towards your infinite light.
We thank you for being with us each day.
Encourage us, we pray, in our struggle
for justice, love and peace.

—Pope Francis, *Laudato Si'*

Acknowledgments

Dorothy Day often quoted Fr. Zosima's words in *The Brothers Karamazov* that "love in practice is a harsh and dreadful thing compared to love in dreams."[1] It was a lesson I learned long ago, as a young Jesuit scholastic serving in Tabora, Tanzania. Having just completed my language studies, I was charged with the care of refugee children. Naively, I believed that simply loving them would suffice. Almost immediately, two of the boys began to fight, and as the fighting escalated, I knew I must intervene. Alas, I could not remember the word for "stop." So, I rushed into our house, found my large dictionary, looked up the Swahili word for "stop," and with a sinking heart, tried to remember how to put it in the imperative plural. I learned, then, the hard grace that love in dreams is not enough.

❖

I want to express my gratitude to Fr. Tom Smolich, SJ, international director of JRS; Andre Atsu, regional director of JRS East Africa; Michael Onyango, country director JRS, Kenya; and my JRS colleagues in Rome, Lesvos, and Paris who reviewed earlier drafts of the book: Fr. Michael Smith, SJ; Fr. Maurice Joyeux, SJ; and Fr. Jean-Marie Carrière, SJ. I owe a great debt of gratitude as well to my oldest friend, Daniel Aseltine, who aided me in the initial editing; Robert Ellsberg, editor-in-chief and publisher of Orbis Books; Maria Angelini, production manager; Nancy Keels, business and production assistant; and Jill Brennan O'Brien, editor, who contributed so much to the final version.

For thirty years I taught the church's social teaching at the Jesuit School of Theology of Santa Clara University and as a visiting professor at Hekima University in Nairobi, Kenya. My students, and even more those whom I was privileged to serve in St. Patrick's African American parish in West Oakland, women incarcerated in the Federal Women's Prison in Dublin, California, and the refugees I served in Tanzania and now serve in Kenya, have taught me the meaning of love in practice. To them, I will always be grateful.

Note

[1] Dorothy Day, "Our Country Passes from Undeclared to Declared War; We Continue Our Christian Pacifist Stand," *Selected Writings*, ed. Robert Ellsberg (Maryknoll, NY: Orbis Books, 1998), 264. See Fyodor Dostoevsky, *The Brothers Karamazov*, trans. Richard Pevear and Larissa Volokhonsky (New York: Vintage Classics, 1990), 58.

Introduction

"How do you say it in your language?" How often we ask this when visiting a new country. But learning a new language is not just about words or translating literally. We learn a language as we learn a game; little by little its rules or grammar become "second nature." Catholic Social Teaching (CST) is a bit like a language, or perhaps better, like the grammar of a language we learn. We speak of familiar things but in a new way, as when Pope Francis urges us to care for "our common home" in the poetry of his namesake, Saint Francis of Assisi.[1] And just as Saint Francis's canticle has inspired believer and nonbeliever alike, so the church's teaching is *Catholic* inasmuch as it is spoken in a particular religious tradition, but also *catholic* (the original Greek means "universal, intended for all").

Yet all too often the church's social teaching remains its "best kept secret."[2] Many scholarly books and articles, to be sure, have explored the origins and development of the church's social teaching. The official *Compendium of the Social Doctrine of the Church* serves as a topical reference; and the principal decrees, encyclicals, and pastoral letters of episcopal conferences have been analyzed in detail. Popular introductions also abound, as do critical commentaries on a wide array of issues. To all of these I am greatly indebted. But there is still work to be done.

For many, church doctrine remains remote from the political currents of our religiously pluralist, secular milieu. In relying on magisterial authority, the *Compendium*'s appeal is largely intramural, while more popular teaching typically distills doctrine in a list of rules or principles that may seem unrelated, or even opposed. How, for instance, can *equal* dignity justify a *preferential* option for the poor, or Pope Benedict XVI's appeal to integral *humanism* be reconciled with Pope Francis's emphasis upon integral *ecology*?

Now rules are critical, but neither scripture nor the church's tradition gives us a simple recipe for living. Rules apply "top down," but we *live* "bottom up." Just as the rules of grammar vanish into speech, so Catholic teaching must be embodied in a way of life. The aim, then, in this little book is modest. I've subtitled it "A User's Guide" because my hope is to show how Catholic *teaching* is not a rule book, but rather a grammar we learn in "our struggle for justice, love, and peace" (*Laudato Si'*, no. 246).

In Part One (Chapters 1–6) I offer a brief introduction to the history, sources, and key themes of the tradition. Part Two (Chapters 7–14) addresses the implications of the church's teaching for such pressing issues as the priority of labor over capital; poverty, racial, and gender bias; the ethics of war and peace; forced migration; and social reconciliation. I conclude with a brief review and an appendix addressing the question of *intrinsic evil*—an often misunderstood term that can be divisive in church politics.

Notes

[1] Pope Francis, *Laudato Si': On Care for Our Common Home*, nos. 1–2.

[2] See Edward P. DeBerri, James E. Hug, Peter J. Henriot, and Michael J. Schultheis, *Catholic Social Teaching: Our Best Kept Secret*, 4th ed. (Maryknoll, NY: Orbis Books, 2003).

Part One

History, Sources,
and Key Themes

1

What Is Catholic Social Teaching?

The church's social teaching is inspired by scripture's prophetic "demands of justice and peace."[1] In the words of scripture scholar John Donahue, "concern for the defenseless in society" is rooted in the very nature of God, "who is defender of the oppressed." Indeed, God "is just not only as lawgiver and Lord of the covenant"—God's "saving deeds are called 'just deeds' because they restore the community when it has been threatened."[2] For the prophets Amos, Isaiah, and Jeremiah, the "core of Israel's faith, knowing God and praising" God, is fulfilled in the works of justice (*sedaqah*).[3] The prophet Isaiah tells us that covenant fidelity demands not ostentatious fasting, but solidarity with the poor and vulnerable:

> Is not this the fast that I choose:
> to loose the bonds of injustice,
> to undo the thongs of the yoke,
> to let the oppressed go free,
> and to break every yoke?

> Is it not to share your bread with the hungry,
> and bring the homeless poor into your
>   house;
> when you see the naked, to cover them,
> and not to hide yourself from your own kin?
> Then your light shall break forth like the
>   dawn,
> and your healing shall spring up quickly;
> your vindicator shall go before you,
> the glory of the Lord shall be your rear
>   guard.
> Then you shall call, and the Lord will an-
>   swer;
> you shall cry for help, and he will say,
>   Here I am. (Isa 58:6–11)

For the prophetic tradition, the welfare of the widow, orphan, and migrant (resident alien) was the measure of covenant fidelity; to forget these vulnerable populations was for Israel to betray its very identity as a covenanted people.[4] For a people born of exile, freedom is thus always "bonded," in Michael Walzer's words—it is always proven true in justice for the marginalized.[5]

For Christians, too, justice is constitutive of evangelization.[6] Jesus turns to Isaiah's words as he begins his own public ministry in Nazareth, revealing God's reign in our midst. Here, in the place of his upbringing, he will consecrate the ordinary. Quoting from Isaiah, Jesus announces: "The Spirit of the Lord is upon me," because God "has anointed me to bring good news to the poor." In covenant fidelity the Lord

God is revealed in responding to the afflictions of the people: releasing captives and restoring sight to the blind, freeing the oppressed, and establishing a year of favor (Jubilee) (Lk 4:16–21). In such acts of justice and in such deeds of loving-kindness and compassion, God's very self is revealed. Here, the divine reign—"good news" for the widow, orphan, and migrant—takes flesh. For the reign of God is truly at hand, even in the One who announces it. "Today," says Jesus, "this scripture has been fulfilled in your hearing" (Lk 4:21).

Luke's Greek speaks of a fulfillment that lasts in history, at once invitation and demand.[7] But how is the good news to be fulfilled for us today? As James reminds us, the divine Word beckons with costly grace. Faith's Word must take flesh in deed for those with ears to hear, eyes to see: "If a brother or sister is naked and lacks daily food, and one of you says to them, 'Go in peace; keep warm and eat your fill,' and yet you do not supply their bodily needs, what is the good of that? So faith by itself, if it has no works, is dead" (Jas 2:15–17). But which works? As we noted above, scripture seldom offers a simple recipe for our moral lives. Much less can we cite chapter and verse to determine a just response to an issue such as forced migration. God's word in scripture is revealed, rather, as a wisdom and a way of life that each generation must incarnate anew. Such is the burden of Catholic social teaching (CST).

CST Is "Catholic" (Capital C)

Since the first modern social encyclical letter, *Rerum novarum*, issued by Pope Leo XIII in 1891, the church's social teaching has guided believers on the way of discipleship, so that, as at Nazareth, God's good news to the poor might be fulfilled even in "our hearing." Today, in our pluralist world, the church seeks to fulfill this evangelical mandate by proclaiming good news not only to believers, but to people of differing religious faiths or none. CST is thus both "capital-C Catholic" (arising from a distinctive religious body of belief) and "small-c catholic" (*catholic* meaning "universal").[8]

Our option for the poor or vulnerable (a theme discussed at greater length in chapter 5), for instance, guides us in recognizing and redressing "multidimensional, overlapping deprivations"[9] of dignity and human rights as we move from general principles, binding on all persons, to concrete applications. Such an option is "small-c catholic" inasmuch as "doing justice" for victims of racial, ethnic, or gender bias is integral to evangelization; yet the gospel demands more:[10] Justice requires *that* we take the victim's side, but *how* we take it will be shaped by our distinctive faith traditions and spiritualities. If they are to "walk humbly" with their God, Christian disciples on the way must also "love tenderly," compassionately (Mic 6:8). For the disciple, love is never less than just, even as "justicing" bears the mark of love.[11] The option for the poor is thus also "capital-C Catholic": the church must not only take the victim's side, it must take it as its own.[12]

In Matthew's Sermon on the Mount, the Beatitudes mark the way of discipleship, blessings not passively received, but to be lived.[13] And much as in Luke's parable of the good Samaritan, the Beatitudes place disciples with the poor, confronting them with the saving irony of the gospel.[14] For in the way of the world, the poor are hardly blessed, their lives little more than unimportant failures. Yet in the Sermon on the Mount, the poor are blest, not because they are poor, but because their affliction cries out to the Just One whose covenant fidelity takes flesh in Christ. They are blessed because of the One who speaks the blessing, Jesus, who incarnates God's blessing for the poor, the seekers of peace, the just. In the blessings of Jesus there is no mundane logic binding blessing and poverty, weal and woe, as indeed there is no logic binding cross and resurrection, save Jesus himself. Finally, it is in him, cursed for us, that the poor are blessed, the naked clothed in mercy, the stranger comforted.

For each disciple living the Beatitudes in solidarity with the poor will be unique. This personal or *religious* option for the poor is finally the wager of a life, as Karl Rahner says, for God has called us by name, "a name which is and can only be unique."[15] The Beatitudes, Pope Francis notes, are thus "the Christian's identity card," calling each uniquely, but all in solidarity, to "the way of holiness . . . the very way of happiness. It is the way that Jesus travelled."[16] These and other insights drawn from the Gospels, church tradition, and Catholic theology demonstrate the distinctively Christian (and even more specifically, Catholic) grounding for CST's emphasis on the preferential option for the poor.

CST Is Also "catholic" (small c)

Such a *living* prophetic word, although "handed on" (Latin: *traditio)* by the church, also speaks to those who share different religious beliefs or none at all. As Pope Francis's encyclical *Laudato Si'* (2015) shows us, the church seeks to translate its beliefs for both a religious and a secular public.[17] The *Catholic* Church, that is, seeks to be *catholic* (universal) in its teaching, drawing not only on the distinctively religious sources of scripture and tradition, but also on secular sources of wisdom, renewed by the experience of every place, culture, and people.[18]

The teaching church is thus always also a learning church,[19] developing as a vital tradition nourished "from below" by the *sensus fidelium* (sense of the faithful) in each new generation.[20] And the learning continues as we respond to the "signs of the times," for example, in Dorothy Day's Catholic Worker Movement; religious NGOs like NETWORK, the Jesuit Refugee Service, and Faith in Action; and ecumenical and interfaith dialogues.[21] Since the patristic era the church developed an ever more refined understanding of its role in the political domain, culminating in the great theological treatises of Saint Thomas Aquinas. In the early modern period the writings of Francisco de Vitoria, Bartolomé de las Casas, Luis de Molina, and Francisco Suárez extended the synthesis of Aquinas to the emerging nation states. The neo-Scholastic (Thomistic) revival initiated by Leo XIII formed the backdrop of the church's modern social teaching.

The Western Enlightenment in the seventeenth and eighteenth centuries bought a new understanding of the political order, at once more individualistic, rationalistic, and radical than the theories of the medieval schoolmen.[22] Since the French Revolution it was recognized that the social, political,

and economic institutions of society were themselves suscep-
tible to deliberate, even violent transformation. Indeed, with
the advent of the Industrial Revolution, the uprooting of the
landed peasantry and their migration into the cities raised a
new social question. The church's modern social teaching thus
begins as Pope Leo XIII's response in *Rerum novarum* (of new
things) to the labor movements; the creation of trade unions;
and the emergence of modern, republican forms of govern-
ment in the late nineteenth century.[23]

Reading the signs of the times, the church's teaching continues to develop in papal encyclicals, apostolic letters, and
homilies; conciliar decrees; synodal documents; and bishops'
statements, such as those of the martyred Archbishop Óscar
Romero. From the late nineteenth century through the middle
of the twentieth century, church teaching appealed principally
to natural law, that is, a common morality grounded in a religiously inspired doctrine of human flourishing. In the wake of
the Second World War the traditional teaching on natural law
was interpreted in the modern idiom of human rights. Pope
John XXIII's encyclical *Pacem in terris* (1963) speaks to "all persons of good will," and two decrees from the Second Vatican
Council, *Gaudium et spes* (1965) and *Dignitatis humanae* (1965),
follow suit. Religious liberty was recognized, and the church
was given a voice to speak to the modern secular world.

Increasingly, the church's teaching is global in scope. Shortly
after the council Pope Paul VI's encyclical *Populorum progressio*
(1967) promoted "integral human development" for all the
world's peoples. Twenty years later Pope John Paul II renewed
Paul VI's call for recognition of the global common good in

Sollicitudo rei socialis (1987). Commemorating the fortieth anniversary of *Populorum progressio*, Pope Benedict XVI's *Caritas in veritate* (2009) criticizes contemporary globalization in light of this rich heritage. Pope Francis's *Laudato Si'* bids us care for all creation as "our common home," while his *Fratelli tutti* (2020) offers a "new vision" of solidarity for our postmodern world.

Catholic social teaching is thus handed on as the *living* faith of those who have gone before us, not the dead faith of the living![24] In the following chapters I show the inner logic and implications of a living tradition rather than quoting extensively from it. Others have treated the documentary heritage at length and in detail. The aim here is modest: to show how the tradition "hangs together" and can be effectively applied, for example, to labor and property, poverty, racism and gender bias, the ethics of war and peace, forced migration, and social reconciliation. In the next chapters let us first briefly consider the terminology and key themes at play in the grammar of "our struggle for justice, love and peace."[25]

Notes

[1] *Compendium of the Social Doctrine of the Church*, no. 3; *Catechism of the Catholic Church*, no. 2419. *"In the social doctrine of the Church can be found the principles for reflection, the criteria for judgment and the directives for action which are the starting point for the promotion of an integral and solidary humanism"* (italics in original) (*Compendium*, no. 7).

[2] John R. Donahue, "Biblical Perspectives on Justice," in *The Faith That Does Justice*, Woodstock Series #2, ed. J. Haughey (New York: Paulist Press, 1977), 69, 73. See idem, *Seek Justice That You May Live: Reflections and Resources on the Bible and Social Justice* (Mahwah, NJ: Paulist Press, 2014).

[3] Donahue, "Biblical Perspectives on Justice," 73–77.

[4] Far from being a litany of arbitrary "thou shalt nots," the Ten Commandments reveal God's salvific "thou shalt": "Today I have set before

you life and death, blessings and curses. Choose *life* so that you and your descendants may live" (Deut 30:19, emphasis added).

⁵ Michael Walzer, *Exodus and Revolution* (New York: Basic Books, 1985), 53, 73–90.

⁶ See Synod of Bishops Second General Assembly (1971), *Justice in the World*, introduction (6).

⁷ Robert J. Karris, "The Gospel According to Luke," in *The New Jerome Biblical Commentary*, 675–721 (London: Geoffrey Chapman, 1995), 690.

⁸ An encyclical is an official papal letter addressed to the church (archbishops, bishops, patriarchs, primates, and Catholic faithful). Since the papacy of Pope John XIII (1958–63), the church's official (magisterial) social teaching embraces not only Catholics but a universal audience. See Pontifical Council for *Compendium of the Social Doctrine of the Church*, nos. 79, 81, 160–63, 221–45, 521–74.

⁹ Multiple Overlapping Deprivation Analysis (MODA) is a tool developed and used by UNICEF to measure and define multidimensional child poverty.

¹⁰ Modern human rights define the moral minimums of justice for complex, religiously pluralist societies; as we shall see in Chapter 6, both biblical justice or covenant fidelity (*sedaqah*) and love (*agape*) demand more.

¹¹ See Gerard Manley Hopkins, "As Kingfishers Catch Fire," in *The Poems of Gerard Manley Hopkins*, 4th ed., ed. W. H. Gardner and H. M. MacKenzie (New York: Oxford University, 1970), 90.

¹² Pope Francis writes, "God shows the poor 'his first mercy.' This divine preference has consequences for the faith life of all Christians, since we are called to have 'this mind' . . . which was in Jesus Christ' (*Phil* 2:5). Inspired by this, the Church has made an option for the poor. . . . This option—as Benedict XVI has taught—'is implicit in our Christian faith in a God who became poor for us, so as to enrich us with his poverty.' This is why I want a Church which is poor and for the poor. . . . We need to let ourselves be evangelized by them. The new evangelization is an invitation to acknowledge the saving power at work in their lives and to put them at the center of the Church's pilgrim way. We are called to find Christ in them, to lend our voice to their causes, but also to be their friends, to listen to them, to speak for them and to embrace the mysterious wisdom which God wishes to share with us through them" (*Evangelii gaudium,* no. 198).

¹³ See *Compendium of the Social Doctrine of the Church*, no. 184.

[14] In John Donahue's words: "The 'poor' in the Bible are almost without exception *powerless* people who experience economic and social deprivation. In both Isaiah and the Psalms the poor are often victims of the injustice of the rich and powerful." See John R. Donahue, SJ, "The Bible and Catholic Social Teaching: Will This Engagement Lead to Marriage?" in *Modern Catholic Social Teaching: Commentaries and Interpretations*, ed. Kenneth R. Himes, 9–40 (Washington, DC: Georgetown University Press, 2004), 22.

[15] Karl Rahner, "On the Question of a Formal Existential Ethics," in *Theological Investigations* 2, trans. Karl H. Kruger, 217–34 (Baltimore: Helicon, 1963), 226–27.

[16] Pope Francis, Homily, Solemnity of All Saints, November 1, 2016; Homily, Solemnity of All Saints, Matthew 5, Verano Cemetery, Rome, November 1, 2015.

[17] See Richard R. Gaillardetz, "The Ecclesiological Foundations of Modern Catholic Social Teaching" in Himes, *Modern Catholic Social Teaching*, 72–98.

[18] In Pope Francis's words, CST must develop "a universal, 'catholic' vision of the unity of our human family and a commitment to the practical solidarity needed to combat the grave inequalities and injustices that mark today's world." Pope Francis, "Address to a Delegation of the 'Villanova University, Philadelphia'" (USA), April 14, 2018. Francis cites *Veritatis gaudium*, no. 1, December 8, 2017. As we shall see in Chapter 6, such a universal vision represents a Rawlsian "overlapping consensus" of distinctive faith traditions.

[19] See *Gaudium et spes*, no. 62; *Lumen gentium*, no. 37; *Compendium of the Social Doctrine of the Church*, nos. 10–11, 79; and Marvin L. Krier Mich, *Catholic Social Teaching and Movements* (Mystic, CT: Twenty-Third Publications, 1998).

[20] See *Gaudium et spes*, no. 4: "The Church has always had the duty of scrutinizing the signs of the times and of interpreting them in the light of the Gospel. Thus, in language intelligible to each generation, she can respond to the perennial questions which men [and women] ask about this present life and the life to come, and about the relationship of the one to the other. We must therefore recognize and understand the world in which we live, its explanations, its longings, and its often dramatic characteristics."

[21] As we shall see in the conclusion of this book, the renewal of CST depends upon learning from the legacy of lay and religious women like

Dorothy Day; Catherine McAuley, RSM; Madeleine Sophie Barat, RSCJ; and Mother Teresa, MC.

[22] See Alexander Passerin d' Entrèves, *Natural Law: An Introduction to Legal Philosophy* (New York: Routledge, 1994), 51–64.

[23] Principal texts: Pope Leo XIII, *Rerum novarum*, May 15, 1891, responded to the great social dislocation of the industrial revolution, defending the rights of workers and their families. Subsequent encyclicals and documents include *Quadragesimo anno* (Pope Pius XI), May 15, 1931, on the necessity for social reform, the social responsibility of ownership, and the rights of workers to employment, just wages, and labor organizations; *Mater et magistra* (Pope John XXIII), May 15, 1961, affirming the priority of the global common good and the rights of the poor; *Pacem in terris* (Pope John XXIII), April 11, 1963, articulating the church's defense of human rights and the relation of justice and peace; *Populorum progressio* (Pope Paul VI), March 26, 1967, treating integral human development in its personal and social aspects, and liberation from structural injustice. See also the following by Pope John Paul II: *Laborem exercens,* September 14, 1981, recognizing the essential subjectivity of human labor, the rights of workers, and the necessity of social and economic transformation; *Sollicitudo rei socialis,* December 30, 1987, renewing Pope Paul VI's criticism of global economic injustice in the modern context; *Centesimus annus*, May 1, 1991, recalling the centenary of *Rerum novarum* and the necessity of moral limitations governing economic transactions; and *Evangelium vitae*, March 30, 1995, addressing a range of moral issues under the rubric of the gospel of life. Pope Benedict XVI's encyclical *Deus Caritas Est* (December 25, 2005), while not falling immediately in the genre of papal CST, outlines themes central to the tradition (see nos. 16ff.; part II). His *Caritas in veritate* (June 29, 2009) offers a rich interpretation and expansion of Pope Paul VI's magisterial treatment of integral and comprehensive development. Finally, Pope Francis's *Evangelii gaudium* (November 24, 2013) addresses many critical moral issues. *Laudato Si'* (May 24, 2015) offers a rich, comprehensive critique of ecological devastationl; and *Fratelli tutti* (October 3, 2020) proposes a new vision of social friendship. Other texts of the CST tradition include Vatican II's *Dignitatis humanae* (*Declaration on Religious Freedom*) (December 7, 1965) and *Gaudium et spes* (*Pastoral Constitution on the Church in Modern World*) (December 7, 1965); *Octogesima adveniens*, the apostolic letter of Pope Paul VI (May 14, 1971), insisting upon the necessity of global

justice in a culturally pluralistic context; *Justice in the World*, the statement of the Synod of Bishops Second General Assembly (November 30, 1971), emphasizing the structural nature of injustice and the integral relation of faith and justice; and Pope Paul VI's apostolic exhortation *Evangelii nuntiandi* (December 8, 1975), recognizing that evangelization implies the promotion of human rights, family life, justice, peace, development, and liberation in both its spiritual and temporal aspects. One must likewise mention Pope Pius XII's topical Christmas messages and numerous statements of synods, regional episcopal conferences, and assemblies.

[24] Jaroslav Pelikan, *The Vindication of Tradition: The 1983 Jefferson Lecture in the Humanities* (New Haven, CT: Yale University Press, 1987), 65. Pelikan writes: "Tradition is the living faith of the dead, traditionalism is the dead faith of the living. And, I suppose I should add, it is traditionalism that gives tradition such a bad name."

[25] Pope Francis, *Laudato Si'*, no. 246.

2

Dignity-in-Solidarity

"The Catholic moral tradition is both *simple* and *sophisticated*," wrote Cardinal Bernardin. "It is *simple* in terms of its basic purpose: the protection and promotion of human dignity, understood as a reflection of the image of God within us. Catholic social ethics, medical ethics, and sexual ethics are all rooted in the nature and dignity of the person." He concludes, "Obviously, this single starting point is then developed in a highly systematic and *sophisticated* fashion so as to address in a detailed way the technological, peace, and justice challenges of our day."[1]

At the heart of modern Catholic social teaching is belief in our innate *dignity* or the sacredness of life.[2] The "Church's social doctrine," says Pope Benedict XVI, is based on our "creation 'in the image of God' (Gen 1:27)," and thus on "the inviolable dignity of the human person."[3] The tradition follows Saint Thomas Aquinas in interpreting the "image of God" (*imago Dei*) as our capacity to act with intelligence and freedom—we are capable, that is, of freely choosing not only what we do, but who we are and what kind of persons we become in relation to others.[4]

Christians, like Jews, believe in God's creation of a "thou" to hear God's word. In the words of the *Compendium of the Social Doctrine of the Church*, "man and woman, because they are free and intelligent, represent the 'thou' created by God."[5] For Muslims, we are God's "viceregents" on earth.[6] Many other religious traditions, including indigenous traditions, likewise affirm what the Preamble to the Universal Declaration of Human Rights (1948) calls our "faith" in the universal "dignity and worth of the human person."[7] The Dalai Lama, for instance, interprets dignity in terms of our "innate capacity" to love, which gives rise to "an ethics of universal responsibility" in Buddhism.[8] But secular reasoning, too, gives us reason to believe. Immanuel Kant describes persons as "ends in themselves"; they can never be treated merely as means to another person's ends.[9] And modern philosopher John Rawls speaks of an "overlapping consensus"[10] of sacred and secular traditions regarding our common faith in dignity. Archbishop Desmond Tutu strikes a similar note: "Apartheid treats human beings, God's children, as if they were less than this. It manipulates persons and treats them as if they were means to some end."[11]

Dignity implies that we have absolute value: dignity does not change like desires, interests, or profits. Dignity is permanent, inalienable, and irreplaceable; no one ever ceases to matter! We cannot give others dignity; nor can their dignity ever be lost or sacrificed, even where it is systemically denied or violated, for example, by forced displacement, racism, or gender or ethnic bias. It follows, then, that we are always worthy of respect *as* irreducibly valuable, independent of what role we play or our social status, religion, gender, class, race, ethnicity, orientation, and so on. Moreover, to say that we *all* have such irreducible value (that dignity is universal) is to say we are *equally* valuable. Dignity extends to everyone alike, so that each person is *uniquely* respected in her concrete "otherness." No one can ever take another's place.[12]

Whether we think of dignity in religious or secular terms, dignity is the basis of moral *solidarity*.[13] Our freedom is bonded by the very value we place upon one another, so that every person is equally worthy of respect and consideration. In a sense, we may say that the human community is present in every person.[14] In Pope Francis's words, "Our being created in the image and likeness of God-Communion calls us to understand ourselves as beings-in-relationship and to live interpersonal relations in solidarity and mutual love."[15] While liberal theorists like Rawls prize the dignity of "mutually disinterested" individuals, and communitarian theorists like Richard Rorty emphasize "local or ethnocentric" solidarities, CST views "dignity-in-solidarity" as an inseparable concept.[16] Archbishop Desmond Tutu captures the theme of dignity-in-solidarity in a single word, *Ubuntu*. *Ubuntu*'s ideal of "social harmony," says Tutu, is "the *summum bonum*—the greatest good." Humanity is never just abstract individuals. Rather, "we belong in a bundle of life. We say, 'a person is a person through other people.' It is not 'I think therefore I am.' It says rather: 'I am human because I belong.' I participate, I share."[17]

In his encyclical *Sollicitudo rei socialis*, Pope John Paul II speaks of promoting such solidarity as at once a duty and a virtue: "This then is not a feeling of vague compassion or shallow distress at the misfortunes of so many people, both near and far. On the contrary, it is a firm and persevering determination to commit oneself to the common good; that is to say to the good of all and of each individual, because we are all really responsible for all."[18] In biblical terms, justice (*sedaqah*) bears fruit in peace/solidarity (*shalom*, signifying not merely the absence of violence, but social harmony and well-being). So too, peace/solidarity is leavened by justice/dignity—social harmony transcends, even as it presumes national, ethnic, or religious membership. As we shall see in Chapter 5, solidarity seeks the well-being not merely of kinfolk but of the widow, orphan, and stranger (those systemically vulnerable).

Dignity-in-solidarity is the wellspring of the tradition,[19] but such general, exceptionless principles must be specified by mediating norms (such as human rights and the common good) as we seek to *do* justice here and now. We may speak, then, of differing levels of authority in church teaching as we proceed from general principles to their concrete application.[20] In market economies, for instance, dignity-in-solidarity demands a living wage, but practical wisdom is necessary to determine what counts as a living wage in particular historical and cultural circumstances.[21]

As in the case of a living wage, dignity appears in local garb, enjoining a *generalized* respect for *concrete* others: We recognize dignity concretely in respecting one another in our distinctive cultural solidarities. As Paulin Hountondji of Benin remarks, "What varies, not only from one culture to another . . . but also within one culture from one period to another and from one class or social group to another, are... the modes of expression of this universal demand for respect and, consequently, the details of the rights considered to be essential and inalienable."[22] So too, for CST. "[It is not] our ambition, nor is it our mission," writes Pope Paul VI, "to utter a unified message" from on high. In the "*living* experience of Christian tradition," says the pope, "Christian communities" must apply "principles of reflection, norms of judgment and directives for action from the social teaching of the Church" to "the situation which is proper to their own country."[23]

Questions for Reflection

1.   When have you most experienced the dignity of those whom you serve, e.g., migrants or prisoners? How have they expressed their dignity, e.g., in stories, proverbs, customs, or rituals? When was their dignity *not* respected? Why?

2.   Alexis de Tocqueville, writing in *Democracy in America* in 1835, was among the first to use the word *individualism,* which he notes is "a calm and considered feeling which disposes each citizen to isolate himself from the mass of his fellows and withdraw into the circle of family and friends; with this little society formed to his taste, he gladly leaves the greater society to look after itself. . . . Each man is forever thrown back on himself alone, and there is danger that he may be shut up in the solitude of his own heart."[24] How does recognition of personal dignity differ from Tocqueville's individualism? How is dignity related to solidarity?

3.   Steve Biko once said, "The greatest weapon in the hand of the oppressor is the mind of the oppressed."[25] One of the effects of extreme oppression or trauma may be interiorized oppression—viewing oneself through the oppressor's

eyes.[26] What are the implications of such interiorized oppression in your ministry or service?

4. Can we give dignity to those whom we serve? Can their dignity ever be lost, forfeited, or sacrificed? A thought experiment: Consider the famous question put by Ivan Karamazov to his brother Alyosha in Dostoevsky's *The Brothers Karamazov*:

> Imagine that you yourself are building the edifice of human destiny with the object of making people happy in the finale, of giving them peace and rest at last, but for that you must inevitably and unavoidably torture just one tiny creature, that same child who was beating her chest with her little fist, and raise your edifice on the foundation of her unrequited tears—would you agree to be the architect on such conditions? Tell me the truth.[27]

How would *you* answer? Now consider the case of torture. Can you imagine any circumstances in which it might be morally justified to torture one who is *not* innocent but guilty, for example, torture to extract information from a terrorist that could save hundreds (or even thousands)? What arguments would you offer to justify your view? How does dignity figure into your answer?

Notes

[1] Joseph Cardinal Bernardin, "The Consistent Ethic of Life and Public Policy," in *A Moral Vision for America*, ed. John P. Langan, SJ (Washington, DC: Georgetown University Press, 1998), 54–55.

[2] See *Compendium of the Social Doctrine of the Church*, nos. 75, 95–114, 132–34, 144–51, 192–96, 244–45, 372–73, 384–92, 398, 421–22, 437, 440–48, 452, 483, 505, 522, 535–37, 553, 576. The *Compendium* speaks of an "integral and solidary humanism" (no. 1). See Pope Francis, *Fratelli tutti*, nos. 213–14, 272–80.

[3] Pope Benedict XVI, *Caritas in veritate*, no. 45.

[4] In *Pacem in terris*, Pope John XXIII appeals to the Thomistic understanding that "any human society, if it is to be well-ordered and productive, must lay down as a foundation this principle, namely, that every human being is a person; that is, his nature is endowed with intelligence and free will" (no. 9). The pope then offers a distinctively religious grounding: "If we look upon the dignity of the human person in the light of divinely revealed truth, we cannot help but esteem it far more highly; for men [and women] are redeemed by the blood of Jesus Christ, they are by grace the children and friends of God and heirs of eternal glory" (no. 10).

[5] *Compendium of the Social Doctrine of the Church*, no. 36.

[6] See *Cairo Declaration on Human Rights in Islam* (August 5, 1990), UN GAOR, World Conference on Human Rights, 4th Session, Agenda Item 5, UN Doc. A/CONF.157/PC/62/Add.18 (1993) [English translation].

[7] *Universal Declaration of Human Rights*, Preamble. See also Pope Francis, *Fratelli tutti*, nos. 213–14, 272–80.

[8] See Elizabeth W. Collier and Charles R. Strain, eds., *Religious and Ethical Perspectives on Global Migration* (Lanham, MD: Lexington Books, 2014), 189. They note that, for the Dalai Lama, our "innate capacity" to love gives rise to "an ethics of universal responsibility" (189) where we "come to see the need to care especially for those members of the human family who suffer most" (His Holiness the Dalai Lama, *Ethics for the New Millennium* [New York: Riverhead Books, 2001], 162–63; also see 64–68).

[9] See Gene Outka, "Respect for Persons," *The Westminster Dictionary of Christian Ethics*, ed. James F. Childress and John MacQuarrie (Philadelphia: Westminster Press, 1986), 541–45. See the correlation of dignity and freedom (primacy of conscience) in Charles Curran, *Catholic Social Teaching: A Historical, Theological, and Ethical Analysis* (Washington, DC: Georgetown University Press, 2002), 76–78.

[10] John Rawls, *Political Liberalism* (New York: Colombia University Press, 2005), 133–73.

[11] Desmond M. Tutu, *Hope and Suffering: Sermons and Speeches*, comp. Mothobi Mutloatse, ed. John Webster (Grand Rapids, MI: Eerdmans, 1983), 160.

[12] Gene Outka, *Agape: An Ethical Analysis* (New Haven, CT: Yale University Press, 1972), 12–13.

[13] See *Compendium of the Social Doctrine of the Church*, nos. 91–103, 150–51, 157, 160, 174, 192–96, 213, 221, 229, 308–9, 321–22, 332–35, 351–76, 417, 433–34, 446–50, 466–75, 486, 556, 580–83.

[14] See Jean-François Lyotard, "The Other's Rights," in *The Politics of Human Rights*, ed. Obrad Savić (London: Verso, 1999), 181–88, at 181. Cf. Immanuel Kant, *The Metaphysical Elements of Justice*, trans. John Ladd (Indianapolis: Bobbs-Merrill, 1965), 34, 52.

[15] Pope Francis, "Sunday Angelus on the Feast of the Most Holy Trinity," May 15, 2016. See Pope Francis, *Fratelli tutti*, nos. 66–68, 114–17.

[16] In *A Theory of Justice*, John Rawls seeks to derive the principles of justice for modern, pluralistic states by subjecting the "mutually disinterested" choice of rational individuals to a "veil of ignorance" (John Rawls, *A Theory of Justice*, rev. ed. [Cambridge: The Belknap Press of Harvard University Press, 1999], 118–23; cf. Rawls, *Political Liberalism*, 13–14). Richard Rorty, conversely, views all ethics as "local and ethnocentric," so that justice appears as "the tradition of a particular community, the consensus of a particular culture" (Richard Rorty, "The Priority of Democracy to Philosophy," in *The Virginia Statute for Religious Freedom: Its Evolution and Consequences in American History*, ed. Merrill D. Peterson and Robert C. Vaughan [New York/Cambridge: Cambridge University Press, 1988], 259).

[17] Desmond M. Tutu, *No Future without Forgiveness* (London: Rider, 1999), 35. Pope Francis cites Archbishop Desmond Tutu as a source of inspiration for *Fratelli tutti* (no. 286).

[18] Pope John Paul II, *Sollicitudo rei socialis*, no. 39.

[19] See Charles Curran, "The Reception of Catholic Social and Economic Teaching in the United States," in *Modern Catholic Social Teaching: Commentaries and Interpretations*, ed. Kenneth R. Himes (Washington, DC: Georgetown University Press, 2004), 469–92.

[20] Authority of principles, norms, and so forth is *internal* if derived from reason and/or revelation. Although we have cogent reasons for saying that dignity is exceptionless, some human rights admit of exceptions, and criteria of judgment depend upon circumstances. Authority is *external* if derived

from office or genre. Thus, encyclicals have greater external authority than papal homilies or episcopal letters. Even homilies or letters, however, may invoke exceptionless or virtually exceptionless principles and norms. See *Compendium of the Social Doctrine of the Church*, no. 8.

[21] The *Compendium*, as a "complete overview" of social doctrine (no. 9), proposes dignity as a fundamental principle, three other general principles deriving from dignity (the common good, subsidiarity, and solidarity), and four fundamental values (truth, freedom, justice, and love) (nos. 108–208). These principles and values "are interrelated and shed light on one another mutually," although in such an overview little is said of the *practical* logic or grammar of their application—our concern here (nos. 8–9, 162–63). So too (as we saw in note 4 above), both Catholic and catholic justifications are offered for the principles and values. Distinguishing, but not separating such justifications lets us speak to both Catholic and catholic (universal) audiences.

[22] Paulin J. Hountondji, "The Master's Voice: Remarks on the Problem of Human Rights in Africa," in *Philosophical Foundations of Human Rights*, intro. Paul Ricoeur (Paris: UNESCO, 1986), 325.

[23] Pope Paul VI, *Octogesima adveniens*, no. 4 (emphasis added).

[24] Alexis de Tocqueville, *Democracy in America,* vol. 2, part. 2, trans. George Lawrence, ed. J. P. Mayer (New York: HarperCollins, 1969), 506.

[25] Steve Biko, *I Write What I Like: Selected Writings* (Chicago: University of Chicago Press, 2002), 92.

[26] See Onora O'Neill, "Justice, Capabilities, and Vulnerabilities," in *Women, Culture, and Development: A Study of Human Capabilities*, ed. Martha C. Nussbaum and Jonathan Glover, 140–52 (Oxford: Clarendon Press, 1995), 142.

[27] Fyodor Dostoevsky, *The Brothers Karamazov*, trans. Richard Pevear and Laarissa Volokhonsky (New York: Vintage Classics, 1990), 245.

3

Human Rights
and Correlative Duties

In Pope John XXIII's *Pacem in terris* and in Pope Paul VI's *Populorum progressio*, dignity-in-solidarity grounds a set of basic claims or entitlements we call rights.[1] In the words of *Pacem in terris*, for example, is clear that each individual "is truly a person," and, as such "has rights and duties, which flow as a direct consequence" from his or her nature."[2] *Human rights* show our respect for the dignity of the human person as an agent and not just as the passive recipient of others' agency—as a means to their ends. In saying persons have absolute value, we implicitly value the prerequisites (conditions or capabilities) of their *acting* as agents.[3] For in order to exercise agency, we must have basic civil-political liberties, basic security from violation or threats and intimidation, and basic welfare: adequate nutrition, drinkable water, shelter, healthcare, education, and employment opportunities.[4] Such basic rights are of paramount importance; they take priority not only over other social aims, but also over other rights that are only means to realize basic rights, for example, private property rights. And because they are necessary for exercising agency, a threat to any basic right imperils others, as threats to basic security imperil civil liberties, and loss of civil liberties threatens security and basic welfare.[5]

Like dignity, such basic claim rights are possessed equally by all persons, independent of social role or standing, disability, gender, religion, race, ethnicity, and so on. Some basic rights are so closely associated with dignity that they are exceptionless (imprescriptible or inviolable); torture, sexual violence, and religious persecution are never permissible. The exercise of other basic rights may be limited for the sake of the common good: parents' religious liberty may be restricted for the sake of their children; speech likely to provoke violence may be proscribed; and freedom of movement can be curtailed during a pandemic. In some strains of the tradition, aggressors threatening the commonweal may forfeit their right to life when all other less violent means of deterrence fail.[6]

Unlike mere liberty rights or privileges, basic human claim rights impose *correlative duties* upon others of both forbearance (what not to do) and performance (what to do).[7] Basic human claim rights thus give rise to both *negative* duties of noninterference and *positive* duties of protection and provision. Pope Benedict XVI insists that rights necessarily "presuppose duties, if they are not to become mere license." Our liberty, that is, is limited not only by others' liberty (freedom *from*), but likewise by positive duties to preserve and protect others' rights (freedom *for* dignity-in-solidarity). For Pope Benedict, duties "reinforce rights and call for their defense and promotion as a task to be undertaken in the service of the common good."[8] And how we defend and promote human rights in serving the common good will depend upon our distinctive social contexts, cultures, resources, and so on, so that general human rights generate culturally specific duties: A right to adequate nutrition for children, for instance, may be guaranteed by equitable employment opportunities for women and childcare in one context and by protecting women's inheritance rights and healthcare in another. Rights must be culturally integrated in our particular narrative traditions, including our religious traditions.

CST thus offers a middle way (*via media*) between differing modern political ideologies: (1) what modern liberal thinkers prize as negative permissive rights—freedom or liberty to do as I please; and (2) what "communitarian" thinkers call the common good—the collective good or customs of a particular ethnic, racial, or national group.[9] CST, by contrast, is *comprehensive* in that it recognizes the full range of civil, social, cultural, and economic rights and correlative duties elaborated in the Universal Declaration of Human Rights (1948). CST is also *integral* inasmuch as the church recognizes the relative priority of the basic human rights necessary for human flourishing (liberties of participation, including religious liberty, basic welfare, and security). Since the papacy of Pope John XXIII (1958–63), the church has thus favored political, social, and economic democracy. The state bears the responsibility for ensuring not only that liberties (civil-political rights) and security are enjoyed, but also that persons' basic needs are satisfied (social, cultural, and economic rights). The market, say popes Benedict and Francis, must be regulated in accordance with the juridical framework of basic human rights and duties.[10]

Questions for Reflection

1.   Milton Friedman was a very influential economist and winner of the Nobel Prize for Economic Sciences in 1976. Consider his critique of CST on economic rights:

> It is, of course, desirable that people get adequate nutrition, but a *right* to adequate nutrition is not a right of the same character or of the same kind as the right to free speech. Free speech is something that everyone can enjoy simultaneously. The only obligation it imposes on other people is not to interfere with it. . . . The situation is very different with a right to adequate nutrition. Everyone cannot simultaneously have the right to adequate food unless there is some cornucopia from which the food comes. . . . The designation of a "right" to food, housing, adequate nutrition and the like to be one a par with the rights of free speech, religion and assembly reflects a collectivist moral vision, a vision that is wholly inconsistent with designating "the dignity of the human person, realized in community with others" as the "criterion against which all aspects of economic life must be measured."[11]

What reasons does Friedman offer for opposing the recognition of the "'right' to food, housing, adequate nutrition and the like"? What are the political and economic implications of his criticism for social policy? How would you respond to his criticism?

2. In your own country of residence, what *legal* protection is given to human rights, both positive and negative, for example, a right to basic healthcare, civil liberties, employment, adequate nutrition, shelter, and education? What *human* rights should be recognized?

3. Why should *participatory* rights of vulnerable populations—such as forced migrants, refugees, indigenous communities, and the disabled—be honored? How are such rights related to the enjoyment, assertion, and enforcement of other basic human rights?

Notes

[1] See *Compendium of the Social Doctrine of the Church*, nos. 95, 148, 151–59, 172–78, 336, 365, 388–89, 401, 421–27, 506.

[2] Pope John XXIII, *Pacem in terris*, no. 9.

[3] *Universal Declaration of Human Rights*, Preamble. Capability theory as developed extensively by Amartya Sen and Martha Nussbaum and incorporated in United Nations Development Programme (UNDP) studies bears significant affinities with the interpretation of basic rights in CST.

[4] See Henry Shue, *Basic Rights: Subsistence, Affluence, and US Foreign Policy* (Princeton, NJ: Princeton University Press, 1980), 5–87. Alan Gewirth terms basic rights "the generic goods of agency," inasmuch as they are presupposed in any reasonable conception of flourishing or perfection (see Alan Gewirth, *Human Rights* [Chicago: University of Chicago Press, 1982], 41–78). Cf. idem, *The Community of Rights* (Chicago: University of Chicago Press, 1996), 31–70.

⁵ In specifying the conditions or capabilities of realizing dignity, basic human rights are both *ends* in themselves and *means* to the realization of other goods, for example, other basic and non-basic human rights.

⁶ The right to life derives from the dignity (sacredness) of life. That is, while dignity can never be sacrificed or forfeited, life may be voluntarily sacrificed, for example, in risking one's life for the common good; and, in some interpretations, it may be forfeited, for example, in the case of prosecuting an unjust war or for capital offenses. We consider the tradition's teaching on just war and capital punishment in Chapter 9. Inspired by the "Gospel of Peace," modern papal teaching has called into question the legitimacy of both war and capital punishment.

⁷ See Wesley Hohfeld, *Fundamental Legal Conceptions* (New Haven, CT: Yale Univesity Press, 1923). Human rights are a species of legal or moral claim rights.

⁸ Pope Benedict XVI, *Caritas in veritate*, no. 43.

⁹ See Pope Francis, *Fratelli tutti*, nos. 163–69.

¹⁰ See ibid., nos. 22, 35; and Pope Francis, *Laudato Si'*, no. 90.

¹¹ Milton Friedman, "Good Ends, Bad Means," in *The Catholic Challenge to the American Economy: Reflections on the US Bishops' Pastoral Letter on Catholic Social Teaching and the US Economy*, ed. Thomas M. Gannon, SJ (New York: Macmillan, 1987), 104–6. (Friedman is citing *Economic Justice for All*, par. 28, which itself refers to *Mater et magistra*, nos. 219–20, and *Gaudium et spes*, no. 63.)

4

The Common Good
and Justice

Although the Catholic Church has historically been suspicious
of negative rights such as religious liberty in the name of the
common good, the modern Catholic tradition respects religious difference (pluralism).[1] Indeed, today, the *common good*
of religiously pluralist/secular societies is defined in terms of
human rights.[2] Thus, it "is agreed that in our time," says Pope
John XXIII, that "the common good is chiefly guaranteed
when personal rights and duties are maintained."[3] The common good will be realized when a comprehensive and integral
rights regime is fittingly implemented, not only nationally, but
globally, for example, in legal conventions and institutions like
the United Nations Refugee Agency.[4]

Our freedom or liberty, then, is positively ordered to the
good of moral community as, in Jacques Maritain's words, "a
whole composed of wholes,"[5] that is, neither a contract of bare
individual agents nor a collectivist subordination of persons
to a class, ethnic group, or nation-state. We realize the good
of moral community in which all share singly, not en masse,

when the "inviolable rights of the human person," including religious liberty, are protected in what John Courtney Murray defines as "public order."[6] Establishing "true religion" by imposing religious duties falls outside the state's responsibility for the common good—now "chiefly guaranteed" in the set of basic, institutional arrangements supporting human rights.[7]

In the words of the conciliar decree *Dignitatis humanae*, in respecting dignity-in-solidarity citizens of faith ought "at all times to refrain from any manner of action which might seem to carry a hint of coercion or of a kind of persuasion that would be dishonorable or unworthy."[8] Freedom, say the council fathers following Murray, is "to be given the fullest possible recognition and should not be curtailed except when and in so far as is necessary," that is, in accordance with the requisites of public order.[9] The church's rapprochement with modern, religious pluralism is thus double edged. For just as distinctive religious beliefs cannot be imposed on the body politic, so too freedom of religious expression is guaranteed. Neither is such expression relegated to the private sphere, for religious liberty anchors the church's prophetic role in civil society as Catholic doctrine is translated into the "catholic" lingua franca of human rights.

Here, too, CST seeks a middle path between the abstract individualism and negative rights of political liberalism and reductive interpretations of the common good, whether Marxist, utilitarian, or communitarian. In our modern, liberal culture, justice is typically thought of as procedural fairness or impartiality in the distribution of social goods and opportunities. Fair outcomes are determined by impartial methods of distribution as the winner of a game is determined by fair rules of play. In CST, conversely, justice is not merely restricted to procedural fairness; fair methods are determined, in part, by just outcomes (consistent with the dignity of persons, their innate rights, and the common good), as seen, for example, in Pope Leo XIII's teaching on the just wage.[10] But neither are persons subordinated to collectivist aims. For *positive* duties of protection and provision give rise to structural imperatives to preserve or establish a rights regime, so that CST's understanding of *justice* integrates both "thin" individual liberties and the "thick" solidaristic responsibility for the common good. CST, we might say, is neither thick nor thin, but extends solidarity to all, especially the most vulnerable.

The Roman Catholic tradition accordingly recognizes a threefold distinction in its teaching on justice: *distributive*, *social*, and *commutative*.[11]

Distributive justice governs the distribution of public social goods to individuals or groups. In CST, "distributive justice . . . implies the right of all persons to share in all those goods which express, support and sustain the public life of society."[12] Distributive justice determines what is owed to each person. In CST, basic human rights define the moral minimum of just distributions; once such rights are satisfied, other criteria, such as non-basic rights, merit, need, social contribution, and achievement come into play.

Social justice governs the activities of individuals and groups in the promotion and protection of the common good. In Pope Pius XI's words, "It is of the very essence of social justice to demand from each individual all that is necessary for the common good."[13] Where basic human rights determine just distributions, correlative *duties* (forbearance, protection, and provision) determine persons' and institutions' responsibility to realize the common good.

Finally, *commutative justice* governs voluntary, contractual relations in the private sphere, such as business or wage contracts. In modern CST, these forms of justice are distinct yet never separate. Our freedom is limited not only by the freedom of others, but by their basic rights and by our correlative duties to preserve and promote the common good. Thus, for Pope Leo XIII, contractual agreement itself is insufficient to determine a just wage; only a living wage for the worker could be just. For Pope Leo and his successors, private property is legitimate, but only insofar as it serves the common good.

In a new millennium marked by massive displacement, systemic deprivation, and degrading inequalities in "new forms of colonialism,"[14] Pope Benedict and Pope Francis seek to safeguard the vulnerable through effective regulative and re-distributive mechanisms. Church teaching is eminently pragmatic, neither denying nor deifying market efficiencies, but subordinating them to "the common good—the good of all people and of the whole person."[15] We must, says Pope Benedict, "civilize the economy." No less than the norms of contractual fidelity (commutative justice), the norms of distributive justice and social justice are internal to a well-ordered market. They are not imposed from without as what economists call externalities. Rather, economic integration—for example, the transnational mobility of capital, finance, and labor—calls for ethical integration, through both state actors and civil society. Solidarity must be expressed within market transactions, as norm and end, lest excessive inequalities imperil the political common good of deliberative democracy. With Pope Benedict's and Pope Francis's "integral humanism,"[16] the development of all, especially the most vulnerable, takes priority over the "superdevelopment" of those who, like the rich man in Luke's parable, neglect their neighbor in need. For *"the primary capital to be safeguarded and valued is . . . the human person in his or her integrity."*[17]

Questions for Reflection

1. The modern philosopher Richard Rorty regards all moral claims as finally "local and ethnocentric" customs—as "the tradition of a particular community, the consensus of a particular culture."[18] How would you respond to Rorty's criticism that neither distributive nor social justice, such as for refugees or forced migrants, is universally binding, but is only relative to particular moral communities and their local or ethnocentric conception of the common good? Are the rights of refugees or children trafficked merely an expression of Western, bourgeois liberalism?

2. How would you respond, in particular, to the claim that women's rights are only the "tradition of a particular community," the "consensus" of Western political culture? Are women's rights human rights? In what sense is gender sensitivity relevant to all basic rights? What arguments would you offer?

3.   Some political theorists today say we must choose between the liberal "politics of *individual* rights" and the communitarian "politics of the *common* good" (the good of a particular social group).[19] How does CST seek a middle ground linking human rights and the common good?

Notes

[1] See *Compendium of the Social Doctrine of the Church*, nos. 164–70, 281, 348, 354, 356, 363–64, 371–72, 388–91, 394, 398, 407–12, 417–18, 422, 432, 434, 437, 441–42, 494.

[2] See Pope John XXIII, *Pacem in terris*, nos. 53–66, 132–41; Vatican II, *Gaudium et spes*, nos. 25–26, 30; *Dignitatis humanae*, nos. 6–7; Pope Paul VI, *Populorum progressio*, nos. 22–24, 43–75; Pope John Paul II, *Sollicitudo rei socialis*, nos. 38–40; Pope Francis, *Fratelli tutti*, nos. 22–24. See also David Hollenbach, *The Common Good and Christian Ethics* (Cambridge: Cambridge University, 2002).

[3] Pope John XXIII, *Pacem in terris,* no. 60. The statement continues: "The chief concern of civil authorities must therefore be to ensure that these rights are acknowledged, respected, coordinated with other rights, defended and promoted, so that in this way each one may more easily carry out his duties." Such a rights-based interpretation permits Pope John to extend the common good globally in *Pacem in terris*, no. 139. See Radio Message of Pope Pius XII, Pentecost, June 1, 1941, AAS XX–XXIII, 1941, 200; cf. Vatican II, *Gaudium et spes*, no. 26, and *Dignitatis humanae*, no. 6.

[4] Conceived analogically, the common good is realized in distinct, yet interrelated, social spheres (for example, family, city, state, and the community of states). The political common good, which preserves public order (justice and peace) in national and global rights regimes, secures the "morality of the depths," that is, dignity and basic rights in modern, pluralist societies. As such, our public, political reasoning does not depend upon a particular, comprehensive conception of the (religious) good in a sacral state. Cf. Pope John XXIII, *Mater et magistra*, no. 65; Henry Shue, *Basic Rights: Subsistence, Affluence, and US Foreign Policy* (Princeton, NJ: Princeton University Press, 1980), 18.

[5] Jacques Maritain, "The Person and the Common Good," in *The Social and the Political Philosophy of Jacques Maritain*, ed. Joseph W. Evans and Leo R. Ward (New York: Charles Scribner's Sons, 1955), 85.

[6] See John Courtney Murray, *We Hold These Truths: Catholic Reflections on the American Proposition* (New York: Sheed and Ward, 1960), 155–74. Cf. idem, "Memo to Cardinal Cushing concerning Contraception Legislation," in *Bridging the Sacred and the Secular: Selected Writings of John Courtney Murray, SJ,* ed. Leon Hooper (Washington, DC: Georgetown University, 1994), 81–86.

[7] See Vatican II, *Dignitatis humanae*, no. 4. Positive correlative duties to preserve and protect agents' basic capabilities (the objects of basic rights) generate such structural imperatives, for example, the state's obligation to guarantee citizens' basic welfare. See Alan Gewirth, *The Community of Rights* (Chicago: University of Chicago Press, 1996), 106–65.

[8] *Dignitatis humanae*, no. 4.

[9] Ibid., no. 7. Cf. John Courtney Murray, "This Matter of Religious Freedom," *America* 112 (January 9, 1965): 40. Murray favors "as much freedom as possible and only as much restriction as necessary."

[10] Pope Leo XIII, *Rerum novarum*, no. 20. See *Compendium of the Social Doctrine of the Church*, nos. 160, 201–3, 332–33, 391, 449, 495.

[11] See Pope Benedict XVI, *Caritas in veritate*, no. 35; *Compendium of the Social Doctrine of the Church*, nos. 160, 201–3. 332–33, 391, 449, 495; Charles Curran, *Catholic Social Teaching, 1891–Present: A Historical, Theological, and Ethical Analysis*, Moral Traditions series (Washington, DC: Georgetown University Press, 2002), 188–98.

[12] David Hollenbach, *Claims in Conflict: Retrieving and Renewing the Catholic Human Rights Tradition* (New York: Paulist Press, 1979), 150.

[13] Ibid., 152.

[14] Pope Francis, address given in Kenya, November 2015.

[15] *Compendium of the Social Doctrine of the Church*, no. 165, cf. nos. 347–48.

[16] The concept of integral humanism will be explored in the next chapter.

[17] Pope Benedict XVI, *Caritas in veritate*, no. 25 (emphasis in original).

[18] Richard Rorty, "The Priority of Democracy to Philosophy," in *The Virginia Statute for Religious Freedom: Its Evolution and Consequences in American*

History, ed. Merrill D. Peterson and Robert C. Vaughan (New York: Cambridge University Press, 1988), 259.

[19] See Michael Sandel, "Introduction," in *Liberalism and Its Critics*, ed. Michael Sandel (New York: New York University Press, 1984), 4, 6, 10.

5

Practical Implications
of
Doing Justice

The foregoing principles and norms of CST govern both personal and social conduct. But CST is not a rulebook. The principles and norms operate much as grammar governs speech. As we have seen, the foundational principles of dignity and solidarity are interpreted in the modern rhetoric of human rights and correlative duties, giving rise to a rights-based conception of the common good. Basic rights, in turn, constitute the moral minimums of a distributively just social order, while correlative duties of social justice, falling on both persons and institutions, promote the political common good. But we must say more if we are to *do* the works of justice. In this chapter we consider further mediating norms that help us determine what justice requires as we seek to implement an integral and comprehensive rights regime in our particular cultures and contexts.

Participation and Subsidiarity

The ethical integration espoused by Pope Benedict XVI and Pope Francis necessarily respects the role of mediating institutions that promote effective and inclusive participation in the associative life of civil society. CST thus recognizes the vital role played by families; civil associations such as churches, synagogues, mosques, and trade unions; nongovernmental organizations (both local and international); and transnational institutions such as the United Nations Refugee Agency.[1] We exercise individual liberty in the context of such complex solidarities so that basic rights of effective *participation* (those most affected should have the greater say) imply *subsidiarity* in realizing the political common good.[2] The principle of subsidiarity specifies the requirements of ethical integration, safeguarding the rights and responsibilities of intermediate associations, so that society is never identified simply with the state. Such institutions should be supported—the root meaning of the Latin word *subsidium*—not supplanted by the state. As Pope Pius XI put it, the state can and should intervene to encourage, supplement, and regulate these intermediate groups.[3]

The Preferential Option for the Poor

Liberties of effective participation and subsidiarity let us share in the political common good. Yet in a world riven by violence and inequity, it is not ethical integration but exclusion that prevails. In doing justice, then, we must struggle to restore the common good—a commitment made concrete in what

Pope John Paul II, inspired by liberation theology, calls "the *option* or *love of preference* for the poor."[4]

And yet, we may object, aren't preferences contrary to justice as fairness? Isn't it unjust to discriminate, even on behalf of the poor? In CST, though, it is precisely the preferential option for the poor (where poverty signifies systemic vulnerability) that determines fairness. Just as a parent cares differently for a sick child than for a well child, so impartial or equal regard for my neighbor's rights justifies preferential attention for my neighbor in distress. Our moral and legal entitlement to *equal respect* or consideration justifies preferential treatment for those whose basic rights are most threatened[5]—in Camus's phrase, our taking "the victim's side."[6] Such a discriminate response is expressed in the moral and legal urgency of basic human rights—the priority of agents' basic rights over other, less exigent claims such as property rights—and in the differing material conditions presumed for realizing those same basic human rights, such as adequate nutrition and healthcare for the poor, especially children.[7]

Restoring the civic *common* good thus justifies a legislative or juridical preference for the least favored in society: poor migrant families, minorities suffering ethnic or racial bias, the disabled, and so on.[8] Securing their basic rights, including their rights to effective, civic participation, marks the legitimacy of our prevailing institutional arrangements. In times of systemic deprivation, violence, and displacement, we must thus ask: (1) Who are the most vulnerable in our midst? Who is missing from the table of deliberation? Whose voice has been silenced by the dominant powers? (2) What are the best means of *general redress*, that is, of securing the basic rights of the poor and marginalized in our particular cultural contexts? 3) What are the best means of *specific redress*, that is, of securing the special rights of victims, here and now? (Refugees, for instance, possess special rights, such as the right to asylum, precisely because their general rights are denied.)[9] Conceived thus, the option for the poor becomes our ethical lens—the way in which, in a religiously pluralist society, we recognize injustice and incrementally implement an integral and comprehensive rights regime. Such a lens, moreover, lets us see the complex interplay of differing moral issues in what Cardinal Bernardin calls a "consistent life ethic."[10] For CST, abortion, euthanasia, forced migration, systemic racism, and endemic poverty all represent fundamental threats to the most vulnerable in our midst.

As the US Catholic bishops conclude in their pastoral letter, "Economic Justice for All":

> The life and dignity of millions of men, women, and children hang in the balance. Decisions must be judged in light of what they do *for* the poor, what they do *to* the poor and what they enable the poor to do *for themselves*. The fundamental moral criterion for all economic decisions, policies, and institutions is this: They must be at the service of *all people, especially the poor.*[11]

Redressing Social Sin

Our option for the poor protects the equal rights of all, especially the most vulnerable. Suppressing such rights, conversely, whether explicitly or through implicit bias, constitutes systemic distortion of our social systems, as seen in white supremacy, xenophobia, gender bias, and so on. Liberation theology offers a theological interpretation of such distortions as *social sin* (also called structural or systemic evil).[12] We may say that social structures or institutions are sinful inasmuch as they systematically suppress human dignity and deny persons' human rights—for example, by state-sponsored torture, official corruption, deprivation of subsistence rights by governments or transnational corporations, and legal or juridical denial of the right to life of the most vulnerable (such as the elderly or unborn) and basic freedoms on the basis of gender, race, ethnicity, disability, sexual orientation, and so forth. Our attention here is drawn to institutions as social actors in their own right. But we may also describe social structures or institutions as sinful inasmuch as they constitute a medium for the transmission of bias that contributes to the denial of dignity and human rights. In his encyclical *Sollicitudo re socialis*, Pope John Paul II thus condemns the "structures of sin" characterized by an "all-consuming desire for profit" and the "thirst for power."[13] Here, our focus is on the institutional transmission of a social ethos marked by systematic bias.

Criticism of social sin implies prophetic *denunciation* of structures that bind and oppress, and prophetic *annunciation* of alternative structures that redress the prevailing injustice.[14] In Pope Francis's words:

Just as goodness tends to spread, the toleration of evil, which is injustice, tends to expand its baneful influence and quietly to undermine any political and social system, no matter how solid it may appear. If every action has its consequences, an evil embedded in the structures of a society has a constant potential for disintegration and death. It is evil crystallized in unjust social structures, which cannot be the basis of hope for a better future.[15]

For Pope Francis, the social grace of solidarity spurs us to redress such sinful structures:

> It also means fighting against the structural causes of poverty and inequality; of the lack of work, land and housing; and of the denial of social and labour rights. It means confronting the destructive effects of the empire of money: forced dislocation, painful emigration, human trafficking, drugs, war, violence and all those realities that many of you suffer and that we are all called upon to transform. Solidarity, understood in its deepest sense, is a way of making history, and this is what the popular movements are doing.[16]

We see systemic bias, both overt and implicit, in the mass incarceration of racial and ethnic minorities in the United States today.[17] Inmates incarcerated in prison or jail number 2.2 million, a 500 percent increase over the last forty years. This is the highest official rate of incarceration in the world (at 731 per 100,000 population).[18] Disaggregating for race and ethnicity shows that "black men are nearly six times as likely to be incarcerated as white men and Hispanic men are 2.3 times as likely. For black men in their thirties, 1 in every 10 is in prison or jail on any given day."[19] As Michelle Alexander argues, our ostensibly impartial, colorblind criminal justice system rationalizes, and effectively erases, its racial and ethnic partiality or bias.[20] In constructing criminal bodies, the state absolves itself.

As we shall see in our discussion of poverty, race, and gender in Chapter 8, the first step of prophetic annunciation, as Dr. Martin Luther King Jr. taught us, is recognizing the nature and scope of systemic racism and white supremacy.[21] As Michelle Alexander, Bryan Stevenson, and Ta-Nehisi Coates argue, solidarity with the victims of the "new Jim Crow" will demand both general and specific redress of our punitive carceral regime—and this redress requires our coming to terms with the "original sin" of racism.[22] In its deepest sense, it will be "a way of making history."[23]

Integral Ecology

Pope Francis's appeal to *integral ecology* in *Laudato Si'* goes hand in hand with the integral humanism (dignity-in-solidarity) at the heart of modern CST (as seen, for example, in Pope Paul VI's appeal for "integral development" in *Octogesima adveniens*).[24] Following Pope Paul, Pope Benedict XVI speaks in *Caritas in veritate* of "integral human development" encompassing the economic, ethical, and spiritual dimensions of authentic human fulfillment.[25] And for Pope Francis, such integral human development is inseparable from our relation to creation itself.[26] Indeed, for Pope Francis, we share in the image of God borne by each creature in its own way so that our solidarity finally extends to all creation.[27] Pope Francis's integral ecology not only enriches integral humanism, but gives us specific mediating norms for realizing it. In doing justice we must (1) recognize the complex, internal relationship of "environmental, economic, and social ecology";[28] (2) preserve solidarities in a "cultural ecology," for example, by safeguarding indigenous cultures;[29] and (3) enhance "the ecology of daily life" so that urban, rural, and family environments may be "setting[s] for a dignified life."[30]

For Pope Francis, the cry of the poor *is* the cry of the earth. Debilitating climate change, systemic loss of biodiversity, endemic pollution, and mass poverty are all, in large part, anthropogenic (of human origin). As Pope Francis insists, ecological degradation disproportionately affects those who are the most vulnerable, yet who are also the least responsible for such degradation, such as "climate refugees"[31] and indigenous peoples. Pope Francis's ethics of integral ecology invites us to a radical assessment that looks to the "roots of the present situation," and not merely to the kind of short-term panaceas so often proposed by the dominant economic powers.[32] For we have betrayed the biblical charge of tilling and tending the garden of our world.

Nature once told a moral tale, but now the world is disenchanted. The book of nature has been divested of any fundamental, metaphysical purpose; nature appears as external to us. Objectified and quantified, it is what we make of it. Since early modernity a purely contingent, instrumental relation has existed between the subject (humans) and object (nature), in what Pope Francis calls a "technocratic paradigm."[33] As a consequence, value resides supremely in the sovereign self; the value of nature is imputed, relative only to our purposes and aims, which are now themselves mere expressions of passion and preferences. And these, as Pope Francis reminds us, are far too often dominated by short-term interest in profit and gain.

Yet, as for his namesake, Saint Francis of Assisi, prophetic annunciation follows denunciation. Pope Francis seeks "an *integral ecology,* one which clearly respects its human and social dimensions."[34] For "an integral ecology is inseparable from the notion of the common good," which demands "a preferential option for the poorest of our brothers and sisters."[35] Environmental, economic, and social ecology, moreover, requires intergenerational solidarity in preserving and protecting our common home. And solidarity extends to our home itself, as integral humanism plays out on the broader canvas of integral ecology, safeguarding ecologies of culture and daily life. For Pope Francis, nature reflects, in its own distinctive and proper way, the image of God, for "the Trinity has left its mark on all creation."[36] Religious belief in creation thus undergirds belief in the *intrinsic* value of all life forms and the natural environment, linking human and natural ecology.

In the secular world of modernity, nature is reduced to a bare, empirical reality that is to be used instrumentally; in contrast, CST affirms the ultimate, intrinsic goodness and beauty of all creation. In Catholic moral theology the natural law is our share in divine providence for all creation; we participate in God's eternal law by caring for all that bears the image of divine beauty and goodness. Indeed, human dignity is realized and manifest precisely in caring for all nature, charged, as the poet Gerard Manley Hopkins said, "with the grandeur of God."[37] Our subjective transcendence is thus *within* nature and expressive *of* nature rather than instrumentally opposed to nature. Here, CST strikes a middle way between a purely human-centered (anthropocentric) ethics and a reductive life-centered (biocentric) ethics, favoring what both African and Eastern theologians call a cosmotheandric ethics of creation.[38]

Questions for Reflection

1. In "Option for the Poor: Old Testament Directives," Carroll Stuhlmueller concludes, "Called to be a compassionate person like God in the Hebrew Scriptures and like Jesus the Messiah, we have no other option than to respond to the outcry and affliction of the poor."[39] Liberation theologians describe such a response as a preferential option for the poor. How would you justify this option for the poor (the systemically vulnerable) when addressing a culturally and religiously diverse audience? Is it simply a charitable religious responsibility, grounded in religious conviction? In particular, how would you respond to the objection that if justice is fairness, any preferences are inherently discriminatory and hence to be judged unfair?

2. What are the implications of the preferential option for the poor (the most vulnerable) for climate refugees or migrants? In your answer, consider the interrelation of integral humanism and integral ecology.

3.   Subsidiarity and effective participation are mediating norms that let us realize the common good in our own particular historical and cultural circumstances. How has the coronavirus pandemic illustrated the necessity of integrating global, national, regional, and local responses? Where has such integration failed, and what might be done to restore the common good (recognizing, always, the ethical implications of the option for the poor, who are often those most affected)?

4.   Western modernity is marked by "disenchantment of the world."[40] Belief in a created order gives way to modern, empirical interpretations of nature as something merely to be measured and manipulated for human purposes. How would you justify belief in the intrinsic value of the nonhuman natural order—as seen, for example, in indigenous respect for ancestral land? How do the differing religious traditions of those you serve justify such belief?

Notes

[1] See Pope Pius XI, *Quadragesimo anno*, nos. 76–87; Pope John XXIII, *Mater et magistra,* 51–77, 122–77; idem, *Pacem in terris*, 140–41; *Compendium of the Social Doctrine of the Church*, nos. 151, 185–91, 214, 252, 263, 281, 293, 321, 351–57, 406–20, 440–43, 449.

[2] For the implications of effective participation, see Henry Shue's analysis in *Basic Rights: Subsistence, Affluence, and US Foreign Policy*, 2nd ed. (Princeton, NJ: Princeton University Press, 1996), 71–78.

[3] Pope Pius XI, *Quadragesimo anno*, nos. 78–80.

[4] Pope John Paul II, *Sollicitudo rei socialis*, no. 42. See also *Compendium of the Social Doctrine of the Church,* nos. 158, 182–449.

[5] Gene Outka, *Agape: An Ethical Analysis* (New Haven, CT: Yale University Press, 1972), 20. Cf. Ronald Dworkin, *Taking Rights Seriously* (Cambridge, MA: Harvard University, 1978), 227.

[6] Albert Camus, *The Plague*, trans. Stuart Gilbert (New York: Alfred A. Knopf, 1960), 230.

[7] See Pope John Paul II, *Sollicitudo rei socialis*, nos. 42–43. Cf. the Medellín and Puebla Conference documents of the Latin American Episcopal Conference.

[8] See Jean Drèze and Amartya Sen, *Hunger and Public Action* (Oxford: Clarendon, 1989), 37–42.

[9] We will revisit these questions in Chapters 8, 10, 11, and 13.

[10] See Joseph Cardinal Bernardin, "The Consistent Ethic of Life and Public Policy," in *A Moral Vision for America*, ed. John P. Langan, SJ (Washington, DC: Georgetown University Press, 1998).

[11] US Catholic Bishops, "Economic Justice for All: Pastoral Letter on Catholic Social Teaching and the US Economy" (Washington, DC: United States Conference of Catholic Bishops, 1986) (emphasis in original).

[12] See *Compendium of the Social Doctrine of the Church,* nos. 117–19, 193, 332, 446.

[13] Pope John Paul II, *Sollicitudo rei socialis*, nos. 36–37.

[14] See Gustavo Gutiérrez, *A Theology of Liberation: Fifteenth Anniversary Edition*, trans. Sister Caridad Inda and John Eagleson (Maryknoll, NY: Orbis Books, 1988), 232ff.

[15] Pope Francis, *Evangelii gaudium*, no. 59.

[16] Pope Francis, "Address to Participants in the World Meeting of Popular Movements," Old Synod Hall, October 28, 2014.

[17] See Bryan Massingale's critical assessment of racism and White supremacy in *Racial Justice and the Catholic Church* (Maryknoll, NY: Orbis Books, 2010).

[18] The Sentencing Project, "Fact Sheet: Trends in US Corrections," August 2020, www.sentencingproject.org.

[19] Ibid.

[20] Michelle Alexander, *The New Jim Crow: Mass Incarceration in the Age of Colorblindness*, rev. ed. (New York: The New Press, 2012), 236–44. See also M. Shawn Copeland, *Enfleshing Freedom: Body, Race, and Being* (Minneapolis, MN: Fortress Press, 2010), 15. For an analogous *mujerista* critique, see Ada María Isasi-Díaz, *En la Lucha / In the Struggle: A Hispanic Women's Liberation Theology* (Minneapolis, MN: Fortress Press, 1993).

²¹ See Martin Luther King Jr., "Letter from Birmingham City Jail," in *A Testament of Hope: The Essential Writings of Martin Luther King Jr.,* ed. James Melvin Washington (San Francisco: Harper and Row, 1986), 289–302.

²² See Alexander, *The New Jim Crow*; Bryan Stevenson, *Just Mercy: A Story of Justice and Redemption* (New York: Spiegel and Grau, 2014); and Ta-Nehisi Coates, "The Black Family in the Age of Mass Incarceration," *The Atlantic* (October 2015).

²³ For imaginative systemic, and specific redress, see Gregory Boyle, *Tattoos on the Heart: The Power of Boundless Compassion* (New York: Free Press, 2010).

²⁴ Pope Paul VI, *Octogesima adveniens,* nos. 31, 52. See also *Compendium of the Social Doctrine of the Church*, nos. 166, 451–87.

²⁵ Pope Benedict XVI, *Caritas in veritate,* no. 11.

²⁶ Pope Francis, *Laudato Si'*, no. 37.

²⁷ Pope Francis writes in *Laudato Si'*: "Believing in one God who is trinitarian communion suggests that the Trinity has left its mark on all creation. Saint Bonaventure . . . teaches us that *each creature bears in itself a specifically Trinitarian structure*, so real that it could be contemplated if only the human gaze were not so partial, dark and fragile" (no. 239).

²⁸ Ibid., nos. 138–42.

²⁹ Ibid., nos. 143–46.

³⁰ Ibid., no. 148; see nos. 147–55.

³¹ That is, people who have been displaced due to the effects of climate change, such as rising sea levels or increasingly catastrophic storms.

³² Pope Francis, *Laudato Si'*, no. 15; see also nos. 14, 32, 53.

³³ Ibid., no. 101; see nos. 106–14, 122.

³⁴ Ibid., no. 137.

³⁵ Ibid., nos. 156, 158; see also nos. 48–49.

³⁶ Ibid., no. 239.

³⁷ See Gerard Manley Hopkins, "God's Grandeur," in *The Poems of Gerard Manley Hopkins*, 4th ed., ed. W. H. Gardner and H. M. MacKenzie (New York: Oxford University Press, 1970), 66.

³⁸ See Engelbert Mveng, "Black African Art as Cosmic Liturgy and Religious Language," in *African Theology en Route*, ed. Kofi Appiah-Kubi and Sergio Torres, Papers from the Pan-African Conference of Third World

Theologians, December 17–23, 1977, Accra, Ghana (Maryknoll, NY: Orbis Books, 1979), 137–42; Laurenti Magesa, *African Religion: The Moral Tradition of Abundant Life* (Maryknoll, NY: Orbis Books, 1997); Bénézet Bujo, *African Theology in Its Social Context*, trans. John O'Donohue (Nairobi, Kenya: St. Paul, 1986); and Raimon Panikkar, *The Cosmotheandric Experience: Emerging Religious Consciousness*, ed. Scott Eastham (Maryknoll, NY: Orbis Books, 1993).

[39] Carroll Stuhlmueller, "Option for the Poor: Old Testament Directives," in *Economic Justice: CTU's Pastoral Commentary on the Bishops' Letter on the Economy*, ed. John Pawlikowski and Donald Senior, 19–27 (Washington, DC: Paulist Press, 1988), 21.

[40] This phrase was borrowed by sociologist Max Weber from Friedrich Schiller.

6

How Is Catholic Social Teaching Distinctively Christian?

The themes we touched on in the previous chapters are both "small-c catholic" (universal in scope) and "capital-C Catholic" (borne by a distinctive religious body of belief). In CST there is no contradiction between a religious ethics and an integral, humanist ethics.[1] As we have argued, respect for dignity and human rights emerges as an "overlapping consensus"[2] of sacred and secular spheres. Such is the case in the Universal Declaration of Human Rights, which affirms our "*faith* . . . in the dignity and worth of the human person," yet offers neither philosophical nor theological justifications.[3] The declaration turns on the distinctive wellsprings of such faith in our varied sacred and secular traditions.[4]

As noted earlier, distinctive religious attitudes and beliefs in catholic/Catholic social teaching (1) support our common faith in dignity and human rights, and (2) enrich such "catholic" faith by inspiring a distinctive Christian/Catholic ethics of discipleship.[5] *Doing* justice (honoring human rights), for believers, thus bears a distinctively Christian imprimatur. "The struggle for human rights," says Jon Sobrino, "is an *in actu* concretization of our faith in God."[6]

Our Common Faith

CST, like the teachings of other religious traditions, underwrites our overlapping consensus between the sacred and the secular. First, CST provides an *ultimate foundation* for faith in human dignity and solidarity. At the heart of Christian ethics is the divine command of love (*agape*), binding us in dignity-in-solidarity. For Pope John XXIII, this dignity derives from our creation in the image of God (*in imago Dei*) and redemption "by the blood of Jesus Christ."[7] In Archbishop Desmond Tutu's words:

> What endows human beings, every single human being without exception, with infinite worth is . . . the fact that each one of us has been created in the image of God. This is something intrinsic. . . . It means that each one of us is a God-carrier, God's viceroy, God's representative. This is why treating anybody as if they were less than this is veritably blasphemous.[8]

So too, for Pope Benedict XVI, our creation in the *imago Dei* testifies to our essentially relational nature: dignity-in-solidarity reflects the divine intimacy of Persons in "*the revealed mystery of the Trinity*."[9] In the doctrine of divine creation, moreover, solidarity embraces our "common home." For Pope

Francis, dignity represents our distinctive share in the intrinsic goodness of *all* nature. For CST, integral humanism presumes integral ecology.

Second, CST provides *motivation* to fulfill the moral demands of human rights and care for creation. Our option for the poor, says Dorothy Day,

> can be proved, if proof is needed, by the doctrines of the Church. We can talk about Christ's Mystical Body, about the vine and the branches, about the "Communion of Saints." But Christ Himself has proved it for us, and no one has to go further than that. For he said that a glass of water given to a beggar was given to Him. He made heaven hinge on the way we act toward Him in His disguise of commonplace, frail, ordinary humanity.[10]

Our religious conviction, Tutu writes, fills us with "a passionate commitment to fight for justice and freedom. We were inspired not by political motives but by our biblical faith."[11] And religious belief inspires care for creation. Pope Francis's appeal to differing spiritualities and faith traditions in *Laudato Si'*—Christian, Muslim, Orthodox, and indigenous—challenges the modern/postmodern worldview of a natural world without value and purpose, a world to be exploited instrumentally for material ends.

Third, CST provides *interpretative resources* (a "moral imaginary") for implementing the ethical demands of integral humanism and integral ecology.[12] Human rights claims do not interpret themselves; they must be embodied or embedded in our particular cultures and narrative traditions. Recalling the very first words of Saint Francis of Assisi's "Hymn to Creation," *Laudato Si'* becomes what the great African theologian Jean-Marc Éla calls a "pedagogy of seeing" the intimate bonds of sisterhood and brotherhood of all creation.[13] In a similar vein Pope Francis appeals to Jesus's parable of the good Samaritan in interpreting the love command (Lk 10:25–37). Pope Francis recalls the familiar tale: When "he saw the wounded man," says Pope Francis, "he did not pass by like the other two . . . but 'he had compassion' (v. 33), . . . that is, his heart, his emotions, were moved! This is the difference."[14] In Luke's Greek, compassion (*esplanchnisthe*) signifies being moved in one's inmost heart. Compassion is not pity bestowed on the poor, says Pope Francis, but instead "means 'suffer with'. The verb indicates that the physique is moved and trembles at the sight of the evil of man. In the gestures and deeds of the Good Samaritan we recognize the merciful acts of God in all of salvation history."[15]

Distinctive religious attitudes and beliefs thus underlie our overlapping consensus regarding integral humanism and integral ecology—a consensus of both sacred and secular publics. Our common faith in dignity and human rights animates religious NGOs such as the Jesuit Refugee Service or Catholic Relief Service, informing the life commitments of believers and nonbelievers alike. CST, as we have argued, is not a recipe, where rules are applied one at a time, but rather a grammar, learned like the rules of a game. Just as an expert player moves effortlessly or naturally in applying the rules, so we do not speak a grammar; rather, grammar lets us speak. Habituated as virtues, or stable dispositions, the rules are realized together, integrally and comprehensively, letting us see, judge, and act aright.[16]

These virtues sustain the *common good* of a rights regime. Solidarity, we saw, is both a duty and a virtue, but so too are justice and our option for the poor—they inspire us, like Luke's Samaritan, to "see and have compassion" as we respond to the suffering and passion of our world. Other virtues, like courage and temperance, strengthen our resolve, while prudence (practical wisdom) guides us in living "bottom up," that is, in *living* justly, as seen in the lives of Dorothy Day, Bishop Óscar Romero, and Mother Teresa.[17]

The Ethics of Discipleship

Yet religious faith transcends the basic demands of such virtues. Distinctive religious justification, motivation, and interpretation in scripture and tradition not only support our *common* faith in dignity and rights, but likewise inspire the disciple's *unique* vocational discernment. As noted above, doing justice in accordance with general principles and mediating norms is fulfilled in loving tenderly, compassionately. As a wisdom and way of life, CST completes itself as the disciple "walks humbly" with God (Mic 6:8). And the way of discipleship is illumined by differing spiritual traditions, such as the Franciscan spirituality of *Laudato Si'* and *Fratelli tutti*. But as a Jesuit, Pope Francis also draws from the well of Ignatian spirituality—in fact, a brief exploration of Saint Ignatius's

Spiritual Exercises can help us to understand the distinctively Christian/Catholic character of CST.[18]

Ignatius marks the way of discipleship in the four "weeks" of exercises of prayerful imagination in discerning the graces of what Kierkegaard once called our ownmost selves.[19] The heritage of CST informs the first week of the Ignatian exercises, as we come to see and respond not only to the sin of the world (including social or structural sin) and the suffering it engenders, but also to the stranger or alien as *neighbor* on our way.[20] The second week, building on the first, interprets this option to respond in intensely personal terms (what the theologian Karl Rahner terms a "formal, existential ethics"[21]). Here the natural virtues (those that may be acquired through our own efforts) are transformed as graced, theological virtues (infused by God).[22] "It is precisely the fire of the Holy Spirit," says Pope Francis, "which leads us to be neighbors to others, to the needy, to so much human misery, to so many problems, to refugees, to displaced people, to those who are suffering."[23]

In the second week of the *Spiritual Exercises* the theological virtue of *love* (*agape*) inspires our personal vocational discernment: our "fundamental option" (our radical response to the love of God revealed in Christ Jesus [see Rom 8:39]). Love binds us in community, a graced solidarity (communion) transcending all national boundaries and borders. The theological virtue of *hope* ("hoping against hope" [Rom 4:18]) motivates us not only to fulfill the demands of justice, but also to respond to the specific invitation of God to "see and have compassion" (Lk 10:33)—to take the victim's side as our own. What is morally good but not required (supererogatory) may be discerned as God's gracious invitation to such acts as accompanying refugees, placing oneself at risk in nonviolent civil disobedience, or waiting for the grace to forgive. Hoping against hope also strengthens us on the way. Migrants' own stories recall the biblical tales of Abraham, Job, Ruth, the prophets, and Christ himself, and the words of Jeremiah ring afresh: "'For surely I know the plans I have for you,' says the Lord, 'plans for your welfare and not for harm, to give you a future with hope'" (Jer 29:11).

Finally, the theological virtue of *faith* tutors our imagination. Grounded in agapeic love and inspired by hope, the story of discipleship takes flesh in the contemplations of the second, third, and fourth weeks of the *Spiritual Exercises*. Here, the love command appears not merely as a general ethical principle, but as an existential invitation. As Jesus concluded in the tale of the Samaritan's loving behavior toward his neighbor, "Go and do likewise!" (Lk 10:37). And contemplation bears fruit in action. As the liberation theologian Gustavo Gutiérrez tells us, "To be a Christian is to draw near, to make oneself a neighbor, not the one I encounter in my journey but the one in whose journey I place myself."[24] The metaphor of neighbor thus becomes a bridge between self and other, a crossing over to the world of the poor, the crucified people. Compassion itself becomes a way of seeing strangers in all their truth.[25] In Pope Francis's words:

Jesus reverses the question of the doctor of the Law, and asks him: "Which of these three, do you think, proved neighbor to the man who fell among the robbers?" (v. 36). The response is completely unequivocal: "The one who showed mercy on him" (v. 37). At the beginning of the parable, for the priest and the Levite, the neighbor was the dying man. At the end, the neighbor is the Samaritan who drew near. Jesus reverses the perspective: do not stand by classifying others by sight who is neighbor and who is not. You can become neighbor to any needy person you meet, and you will know that you have compassion in your heart, that is, whether you have the capacity to suffer with the other.[26]

The love command *is* Love's command, configuring our story, little by little, as gospel.[27] And in becoming neighbor, we meet Jesus in the miracle of the ordinary. As Gutiérrez writes:

> The poor constitute a world of their own. Commitment to the poor means entering, and in some cases remaining in, that universe with a much clearer awareness; it means being one of its inhabitants, looking upon it as a place of residence and not simply of work. It does not mean going into that world by the hour to bear witness to the gospel, but rather emerging from within it each morning in order to proclaim the good news to every human being.[28]

Such living into blessing is a hard grace:

> It is necessary, therefore, to undertake this commitment although knowing in advance that the situation of the poor will almost certainly overstrain the human capacity for solidarity. The will to live in the world of the poor can therefore only follow an asymptotic curve: a constantly closer approach that can, however, never reach the point of real identification with the life of the poor. Not even the surrender of their lives brings individuals to that goal, despite the ultimacy of the witness they give.[29]

And no one is spared this hard grace. The poor, too, must "pass over" to the side of the suffering in their midst. I think of a woman named Mama Kasim, caring daily for her seven-year-old child with cerebral palsy in Kenya's Kakuma refugee camp. Although such severely disabled children are sometimes abandoned, this mother's love bears eloquent witness to "the saving power" of God at work in her life.[30] Mama Kasim is not defeated.

We must, says Pope Francis, "be evangelized" by the poor; they are "at the centre of the Church's pilgrim way."[31] For Pope Francis, disciples must become the blessing they receive, tracing the way of a crucified love in Ignatius's third week. This part of the *Spiritual Exercises* confirms our passing over to the crucified One amid the crucified. Here we come to see, as if for the first time, the lesson of love: that love suffers because it is love and nothing but love. And it is not only the labor, but the supreme risk of a life. What the Lord requires, then, is finally not this or that deed of love, but the deed of our very selves. What is commanded, says Rahner, is "oneself demanded in the concreteness of one's heart."[32] The words of the Beatitudes must be proven true in the one who hears them as, little by little, one is incorporated into the blessed community, the body of Christ (1 Cor 12:12–30).

The fourth week of contemplating Jesus's resurrection is not just a "grace note." Easter is not merely the final, supreme miracle—the last, unearthly event of Jesus's life. No, Easter is the truth of Calvary, of crucified love. It is the hermeneutic of the suffering and passion of the world, where the flawed words of our stories are gradually made gospel.

As Isaiah tells us, we thought we had "labored in vain" (Isa 49:4). Yet all the while God labors in us, Christ is in the ten thousand places of *our* labor, in the silence of *our* Calvaries, as the word of love.[33] In Matthew's Gospel the Beatitudes recur in the story of the last judgment, where the labor of a life, the religious option for the poor, is revealed as Christ's labor in and for us. Thinking we are the hosts in doing to these "least," we become Christ's guests at the eschatological feast. Those who "hunger and thirst for righteousness" are filled (Mt 5:6):

> Come, you that are blessed by my Father, inherit the kingdom prepared for you from the foundation of the world; for I was hungry and you gave me food, I was thirsty and you gave me something to drink, I was a stranger and you welcomed me, I was naked and you gave me clothing, I was sick and you took care of me, I was in prison and you visited me. (Mt 25:34–36)

Questions for Reflection

1. How does religious difference come into play when promoting the ideals and values of an integral humanism? Consider, in particular, the relation of love (charity) and justice. If we take the biblical virtue of love seriously, can we separate love and justice, as in the phrase: "It's a question of justice, not charity"?

2. In modern religiously pluralist societies, religion is often consigned to the private sphere. What public and political role, if any, should the church or other religious institutions play? What makes a religious voice credible in the public square?

3. What resources from your own religious or secular traditions inform your commitments to "draw near" to those on the margins? What stories are particularly relevant for you?

4. What value do you see (even if you are yourself agnostic) in understanding the religious convictions, stories, rituals, and so forth, of those whom you serve?

Notes

[1] See *Compendium of the Social Doctrine of the Church,* nos. 1–19, 72–86, 206.

[2] John Rawls, *Political Liberalism* (New York: Colombia University Press, 2005), 133–73.

[3] *Universal Declaration of Human Rights*, Preamble.

[4] See David Little and Sumner B. Twiss, *Comparative Religious Ethics: A New Method* (San Francisco: Harper and Row, 1978); Joseph Runzo, Nancy M. Martin, and Arvind Sharma, eds., *Human Rights and Responsibilities in the World Religions,* The Library of Global Ethics and Religion, vol. 4 (Oxford: Oneworld, 2002).

[5] Duties and virtues of discipleship are distinctively, yet not uniquely, Christian. Believers of other faiths or none may fulfill the spirit, if not the letter of the law, for example, in "seeing and having compassion" like Luke's Samaritan (Lk 10:33). See the Conclusion of this book.

[6] Jon Sobrino, *The Spirituality of Liberation: Toward Political Holiness*, trans. Robert R. Barr (Maryknoll, NY: Orbis Books, 1988), 104.

[7] Pope John XXIII, *Pacem in terris*, nos. 9–10.

[8] Desmond M. Tutu, *No Future without Forgiveness* (London: Rider, 1999), 11.

[9] Pope Benedict XVI, *Caritas in veritate*, no. 54 (emphasis in original).

[10] Dorothy Day, *Selected Writings*, ed. Robert Ellsberg (Maryknoll, NY: Orbis Books, 1998), 96–97.

[11] Tutu, *No Future without Forgiveness*, 11.

[12] See Charles Taylor, *Modern Social Imaginaries*, ed. Dilip Parameshwar Gaonkar, Benjamin Lee, Jane Kramer, and Michael Warner (Durham, NC: Duke University Press, 2004).

[13] Jean-Marc Éla, "Christianity and Liberation in Africa," in *Paths of African Theology*, ed. Rosino Gibellini, 136–53 (Maryknoll, NY: Orbis Books, 1994), 143.

[14] Pope Francis, General Audience, St. Peter's Square, April 27, 2016.

[15] Ibid.

[16] Cardinal Joseph Cardijn's exhortation to "see, judge, act" has inspired generations of Christians to engage in (1) experience/discernment; (2) social analysis/critical theological reflection; and (3) personal/social action. See Pope Francis, *Laudato Si'*, no. 15; Erin M. Brigham, *See, Judge, Act: Catholic Social Teaching and Service Learning*, rev. ed. (Winona, MN: Anselm Academic, 2018); Thomas Massaro, SJ, *Living Justice: Catholic Social Teaching in Action*, 3rd classroom ed. (Lanham, MD: Rowman and Littlefield, 2016); Edward P. DeBerri, James E. Hug, Peter J. Henriot, Michael J. Schultheis, *Catholic Social Teaching: Our Best Kept Secret*, 4th rev. ed. (Maryknoll, NY: Orbis Books, 2003).

[17] For Aristotle and Aquinas, virtue signifies excellence in living well and doing well (happiness or flourishing). The virtue of justice is other regarding, so that living justly implies civic friendship, civility, and so on.

[18] *The Spiritual Exercises of Saint Ignatius: A Translation and Commentary*, George E. Ganss, SJ (St. Louis: Institute of Jesuit Sources, 1992). See also

John C. Endres and Elizabeth Liebert, *A Retreat with the Psalms: Resources for Personal and Communal Prayer* (Mahwah, NJ: Paulist Press, 2001).

[19] See Søren Kierkegaard, *The Concept of Irony*, trans. Howard V. Hong and Edna H. Hong, *Kierkegaard's Writings*, vol. 2 (Princeton, NJ: Princeton University Press, 1992), 272–323; see also Kierkegaard, *Either/Or*, Part II, trans. Howard V. Hong and Edna H. Hong, *Kierkegaard's Writings*, vol. 4 (Princeton, NJ: Princeton University Press, 1987).

[20] The "Colloquy" of the "First Exercise" places us before the crucified Lord. In Dean Brackley's reading of the *Exercises*, we respond to the crucified Lord in the crucified people (*Spiritual Exercises*, no. 53). See Dean Brackley, SJ, *The Call to Discernment in Troubled Times: New Perspectives on the Transformative Wisdom of Ignatius of Loyola* (New York: Crossroad, 2004), 40–41; Jon Sobrino, "Companions of Jesus," in Jon Sobrino, Ignacio Ellacuría, et al., *Companions of Jesus: The Jesuit Martyrs of El Salvador* (Maryknoll, NY: Orbis Books, 1990), 3–56.

[21] For Rahner, a "formal, existential" ethics of discernment in the second week presumes, even as it transcends, the *general* ethical principles and norms at play in the first week. The theological virtues perfect the "essential" ethics of natural virtue: the theological virtue of love justifies the disciple's election; the theological virtue of hope motivates the disciple following the crucified Lord; and the theological virtue of faith reveals the disciple's way. As developed here, an "essential ethics of norms and order" allows for multiple comprehensive conceptions of the good and hence need not succumb to postmodern critiques of essentialism. See Karl Rahner, "On the Question of a Formal Existential Ethics," in *Theological Investigations 2*, trans. Karl H. Kruger, 217–34 (Baltimore: Helicon, 1963), 228. See also Karl Rahner, "The 'Commandment' of Love in Relation to the Other Commandments," in *Theological Investigations 5*, trans. Karl H. Kruger (New York: Seabury, 1966), 439–59; "Theology of Freedom," in *Theological Investigations 6*, trans. Karl and Boniface Kruger (New York: Seabury, 1974), 178–96; and "Reflections on the Unity of the Love of Neighbour and the Love of God," in *Theological Investigations 6*, 231–49.

[22] Saint Paul speaks of the theological virtues in 1 Corinthians 13:1–13; Thomas Aquinas interprets them in his *Summa Theologiae*: *ST* I–II, Q. 62. Cf. Saint Ignatius's "Rules for Thinking, Judging, and Feeling with the Church," no. 363 (*Spiritual Exercises*, no. 135).

[23] Pope Francis, "Angelus Address," August 14, 2016. See Pope Francis, *Fratelli tutti*, nos. 88–100.

[24] Gustavo Gutiérrez, "Toward a Theology of Liberation" (July 1968), trans. Alfred T. Hennelly, in *Liberation Theology: A Documentary History*, ed. Alfred T. Hennelly, 62–76 (Maryknoll, NY: Orbis Books, 1990), 74.

[25] Simone Weil, "Reflections on the Right Use of School Studies with a View to the Love of God," in *Waiting for God*, trans. Emma Craufurd, 105–16 (New York: G. P. Putnam's Sons, 1951), 115.

[26] Pope Francis, "General Audience," Saint Peter's Square, April 27, 2016. See Pope Francis, *Fratelli tutti*, nos. 56–86.

[27] See Luke 6:27–37; Luke 10:25–37; Matthew 22:36–40; Mark 12:28–34; John 13:34–35; 15:9–17.

[28] Gustavo Gutiérrez, *We Drink from Our Own Wells* (Maryknoll, NY: Orbis Books, 2003), 125–26.

[29] Ibid.

[30] Pope Francis, *Evangelii gaudium,* no. 198.

[31] Ibid.

[32] Rahner, "The 'Commandment' of Love in Relation to the Other Commandments," 453.

[33] Gerard Manley Hopkins writes: "Christ plays in ten thousand places, / Lovely in limbs, and lovely in eyes not his / To the Father through the features of men's faces." ("As Kingfishers Catch Fire," in *The Poems of Gerard Manley Hopkins*, 4th ed., ed. W. H. Gardner and H. M. MacKenzie [New York: Oxford University Press, 1970], 90).

Part Two

Applications

7

Labor and the Economy

The Priority of Labor over Capital

As we turn from the key themes of CST to their application, it is fitting that we begin with the rights of workers and their families.[1] As we noted in the Introduction, the Catholic Church's social critique was forged in the crucible of the modern labor movement. Teaching, of course, begins with learning—and in the second half of the nineteenth century, the vibrant "social Catholicism" of Wilhelm Emmanuel von Ketteler, Albert de Mun, René de La Tour du Pin, and members of the Fribourg Union set the stage for the church's response to the new social question related to labor, liberalism, and social injustice. Inspired by Bishop Ketteler, whom Pope Leo XIII called his "great predecessor," *Rerum novarum* (1891) defended the rights of the industrial proletariat; Pope Leo's successors, Pope Pius XI and Pope Pius XII, followed suit.[2] Pope John XXIII spoke to the modern world in the language of human rights, and in the wake of the Second Vatican Council, Pope Paul VI applied CST globally, treating labor in the context of integral human development.

Perhaps no pope, though, has spoken more cogently of labor than Pope John Paul II, a former laborer himself. For Pope John Paul II, the dignity and rights of laborers serve as a privileged expression of human agency in promoting the common good. Indeed, work represents our participation in divine creativity, not only through economic activity, but also through art and culture. Far from being punishment for original sin, labor expresses the *imago Dei*. Work "is not only good in the sense that it is useful or something to enjoy; it is also good as being something worthy, that is to say, something that corresponds to man's dignity." For Pope John Paul II, the dignity of work rests in its subjective dimension, rather than in the objective type of work done. As "the subject of work," persons must never be treated merely as means, as if they were "an instrument of production"; labor assumes priority over capital.[3]

The dignity of workers (as ends in themselves) generates both rights and duties. In accordance with the norms of distributive justice, every person is entitled to the opportunity of productive employment and exercise of economic initiative as a means of participating effectively in society. Further rights deriving from a person's dignity include a just remuneration for work done, adequate healthcare and insurance, a safe working environment, and protection of the liberty to form unions and other associative liberties. And as we saw, basic rights impose correlative duties to contribute to the common good. In accordance with the norms of social justice, a person, Pope John Paul II writes,

must work out of regard for others, especially his
own family, but also for the society he belongs to, the
country of which he is a child, and the whole human
family of which he is a member, since he is the heir to
the work of generations and at the same time a sharer
in building the future of those who will come after him
in the succession of history.[4]

Positive duties of provision and protection, moreover, generate structural imperatives borne by social institutions. In
conjunction with the private sector, the state must provide
for such needs as equitable employment, equal opportunity,
a living wage, a safe workplace, and adequate healthcare.
Concurrently, unions, religious institutions, NGOs, and
international organizations such as the ILO (International
Labor Organization) safeguard effective representation, due
process, and equal treatment, such as respect for women's
employment rights.

Private Property

Expressed in the doctrine of human rights, the personal-
ist ends of social institutions militate against all totalizing
ideologies. Pope Leo XIII insists that persons "precede the
state," while Pope Pius XI writes that "society is for man and
not vice versa."[5] Inspired by the biblical mandate of faithful
stewardship of the earth's riches,[6] CST on property thus seeks
to offer a middle way between the liberalistic individualism

of laissez-faire capitalism and the collectivist ideology of Marxist-Leninist communism.[7]

Here, as in the case of labor, doctrine develops from the bottom up, as the listening church responds to new social questions. (Wisdom is always in the making!) Pope Leo XIII's *Rerum novarum* denounced the radical socialization of means of production yet also recognized the natural right of the industrial proletariat to just remuneration and retention of the fruits of labor. "The utter poverty of the masses" was to be ameliorated through a broad dissemination of the natural right to (consumptive and productive) property.[8] Pope Pius XI's *Quadragesimo anno* defended the institution of private property as a bulwark against undue restrictions of personal liberty and as an effective means of satisfying basic human needs.[9] For Pope Pius XI and his successor, Pope Pius XII, the accumulation of wealth and property "remains subordinated to the natural scope of material goods and cannot emancipate itself from the first and fundamental right which concedes their use to all."[10]

Like his predecessors, Pope John XXIII derives the right to private property from the fruitfulness of work, while affirming the common finality of material goods. *Mater et magistra* defends the right to hold private property as a safeguard and stimulus for the exercise of freedom and the rights of the human person.[11] Yet the *personal* right to property presupposes the correlative *social* duty of ensuring not merely a broader, but a more equitable distribution of property rights so that all in the community can develop and perfect themselves.[12] In *Pacem in terris*, Pope John XXIII insists that the right to private property is qualified by other universal human rights deriving from the inherent dignity of the human person.[13]

The *Pastoral Constitution on the Church in the Modern World* (*Gaudium et spes*) of Vatican II reaffirms that private ownership, as an expression of personality, represents an extension of human freedom offering an incentive for persons to fulfill their function and duty in society and in the economy. Yet property's social quality, deriving from the law of the communal purpose of earthly goods, subordinates private property rights to the global common good.[14] In *Populorum progressio*, Pope Paul VI treats property rights in terms of integral development: ownership must foster the good of the whole person and of every person, especially the victims of oppressive social structures originating in the abuses of ownership and power.[15]

In *Laborem exercens*, Pope John Paul II argues that the only legitimate title to capital is that it should serve labor, promoting the solidarity of laborers and of the poor.[16] In *Sollicitudo rei socialis* he insists that the right to property bears a "social mortgage" deriving from the priority of the subjectivity of human labor over capital.[17] In accordance with the principle of subsidiarity, Pope John Paul II thus recognizes not only the legitimacy of labor unions and of socializing certain means of production, but of workers' participation in policy formation, management, and ownership.[18] With the demise of European communism, *Centesimus annus* (1991) commemorates the centennial of *Rerum novarum* by reaffirming "*a society of free work, of enterprise and of participation*."[19]

Such a juridical framework is not utopian. In a world where scarcity and limited altruism still prevail, economic inequalities are permissible, but with a proviso: they must serve the rights-based common good. Consistent with the dictates of distributive and social justice, basic human rights, including the participatory rights of the poor or systemically vulnerable, must be satisfied prior to non-basic rights or other distributive criteria.[20] The "social mortgage" remains! Decrying the enduring scandal of poverty in our world, Pope Francis recalls the words of Saint John Chrysostom: "Not to share one's goods with the poor is to rob them and to deprive them of life. It is not our goods that we possess, but theirs."[21]

Questions for Reflection

1.   Nobel Prize–winning economist Milton Friedman argues that "there is one and only one social responsibility of business—to use its resources and engage in activities designed to increase its profits so long as it stays within the rules of the game, which is to say, engages in open and free competition without deception or fraud."[22] Other business ethicists have criticized Friedman's shareholder theory for failing to account for the many "stakeholders" affected, directly and indirectly, by corporate policies. From the perspective of CST on the priority of labor, how would you respond?

2.   The Christian tradition has often interpreted work as punishment for original sin (Gen 3:17–19). Even when well remunerated, work is often viewed as a means of satisfying private interests (work, that is, as an expression of what Robert Bellah calls "utilitarian individualism"[23]). Yet for Pope John Paul II, work is something worthy, that is to say, something that corresponds to our dignity. In what sense does

work express human creativity? What are the implications of his teaching for protecting workers' rights to dignified work in the case of those who are unemployed or underemployed?

3.   Contemporary libertarian philosopher Robert Nozick argues in a Lockean vein that the just acquisition or transfer of property is sacrosanct, so that socially mandated redistribution—for example, social welfare policy—represents a fundamental violation of individual rights. For Nozick, even vast inequalities would be justified if property and wealth were legitimately acquired.[24] How might Pope John Paul II respond in light of his belief that private property entitlements bear a "social mortgage"? When do growing inequalities undermine a regime of basic rights, for example, to effective democratic participation?

4.   Today, many countries in the global South are heavily indebted to banks and financial institutions like the International Monetary Fund (IMF) and World Bank. In times of unforeseen crisis, like the coronavirus pandemic, some argue that their debts should be forgiven or remitted. How would you respond in light of CST?

Notes

[1] See *Compendium of the Social Doctrine of the Church,* nos. 255–66, 270–310, 335.

[2] See Marvin L. Krier Mich, *Catholic Social Teaching and Movements* (Mystic, CT: Twenty-Third Publications, 1998), 7.

[3] Pope John Paul II, *Laborem exercens*, nos. 9, 22, 7; see also nos. 4, 6, 12, 13.

[4] Ibid., no.16.

[5] Pope Leo XIII, *Rerum novarum*, no. 7; Pope Pius XI, *Divini redemptoris*, no. 29.

[6] Scripture recognizes private property, yet it subordinates property claims to God's salvific purposes. The theme of faithful stewardship of the earth's riches (Mt 25:14–30; Lk 16:1–15; Lk 19:12–27; 1 Cor 4:7) is elaborated in the patristic period (see Basil, *Hom.* I in Ps 14:5; John Chrysostom, *Hom.* in 1 Tim 11, *De Lazaro*, 2.4, 6ff., and *Hom.* in Rom 11:5). Augustine's belief that private property was an institution of positive rather than divine law (*In Joann. Ev.* 6.25–26, *Ep.* 93.12.50) was systematically elaborated in the writings of Thomas Aquinas. The natural law, for Aquinas, decreed the common finality of external goods and the general "right" (*dominium*) over their use; private property rights arise as a "positive" specification "added to natural law" for our benefit and perfection (*Summa Theologiae* II-II, Q. 66, art. 2 (cf. *ST* I-II, Q. 94, art. 5; *ST* II-II, Q. 32, art. 5; *De Regimine Principum*, Bk. 1, chaps. 15, 17). The positive right to private property thus presumes the natural obligation of securing the common good of the community. Indeed, Aquinas admits that "in cases of necessity everything is common property" (*ST* II-II, Q. 66, art. 7). The Thomistic heritage was transmitted in the Renaissance through the writings of the Spanish Scholastics Vitoria, Molina, and Suárez.

[7] See *Compendium of the Social Doctrine of the* Church, nos. 171–81.

[8] Pope Leo XIII, *Rerum novarum*, nos. 1, 22, 33, 43–47.

[9] Pope Pius XI, *Quadragesimo anno*, nos. 45–51.

[10] Pope Pius XII, *Acta Apostolicae Sedis* 33, 198–99; cf. Pope Pius XI, *Quadragesimo anno*, nos. 49, 57–58, 61, 78–80, 114–15 and Pope Pius XII, *La solennità,* nos. 31–33.

[11] See Pope John XXIII, *Mater et magistra*, nos. 109–12, 119.

[12] Ibid., no. 67.

[13] See Pope John XXIII, *Pacem in terris*, nos. 9, 21–22, 60, 63, 84, 139. Cf. *Mater et magistra*, nos. 65, 75, 77, 92–93, 97, 104, 120.

[14] See Vatican II, *Gaudium et spes*, nos. 69–71.

[15] See Pope Paul VI, *Populorum progressio*, nos. 14, 21–24, 26, 48–49; see also *Octogesima adveniens*, nos. 43–44; World Synod of Catholic Bishops, *Justice in the World* (1971), nos. 14–16.

[16] Pope John Paul II, *Laborem exercens*, nos. 32–37, 63–69; *Sollicitudo rei socialis*, nos. 28–31, 39.

[17] Pope John Paul II, *Sollicitudo rei socialis*, no. 42.

[18] See Pope John Paul II, *Laborem exercens*, nos. 64–69, 94–10, 102.

[19] Pope John Paul II, *Centesimus annus*, no. 35; see also nos. 6, 11–13, 19, 24, 30–43, 48, 61.

[20] In John Rawls's interpretation of procedural justice the "difference principle" provides that inequalities are justified if they redound to the greatest benefit of the least advantaged; CST interprets the "greatest benefit" materially. CST does not directly address Rawls's critique, but we might infer from the duties correlative to basic human rights that economic inequalities are justified only if (a) they do not violate basic human rights, including the right to effective participation (degrading inequalities are never permissible); and (b) they derive from social arrangements that best preserve and protect such rights. (See John Rawls, *Political Liberalism* [New York: Columbia University Press, 1993], iv–viii; 5–6; 291). Cf. Rawls's interpretation of David Hume's circumstances of justice in John Rawls, *A Theory of Justice*, rev . ed. (Cambridge: The Belknap Press of Harvard University Press, 1999), 109–10.

[21] Pope Francis, Audience with Ambassadors (regarding financial reform), May 16, 2013. See Pope Francis, *Fratelli tutti*, nos. 118–20.

[22] Milton Friedman, "The Social Responsibility of Business Is to Increase Its Profits," in *Ethical Theory and Business*, 8th ed., ed. Tom L. Beauchamp, Norman E. Bowie, and Denis G. Arnold (Upper Saddle River, NJ: Pearson, 2009), 55.

[23] See Robert N. Bellah, "Is There a Common American Culture?" *The Journal for the American Academy of Religion* 66, no. 3 (Fall 1998): 613–25.

[24] Robert Nozick, *Anarchy, State, and Utopia* (Oxford: Basil Blackwell, 1974).

8

Poverty, Racism, and Gender Bias

In Robert Bolt's play *A Man for All Seasons*, the aging Cardinal Wolsey rebukes Sir Thomas More: "You're a constant regret to me, Thomas. If you could just see the facts flat on, without that horrible moral squint; with just a little common sense, you could have been a statesman."[1] For Wolsey, the "facts" of savvy politics leave little room for More's moral scruples. And yet, modern hermeneutics reminds us, we seldom see the facts flat on. Invariably we bring, often tacitly, our own interpretative perspectives—our common sense—to bear.

CST, as we saw in Chapters 1–6, is our "horrible moral squint"—our way of discerning the signs of the times. And such teaching often goes against the grain. For many, everyday morality typifies poverty as the result of life's natural lottery—thus our wealth is unencumbered, our privilege deserved. And if privilege is deserved, the poor are, at best, objects of charity. As Ralph Waldo Emerson once remarked, "Do not tell me, as a good man did today, of my obligation to put all poor men in good situations. Are they my poor?"[2]

Indeed, it is only a step further to say that, like wealth, poverty is deserved. Sociologist Robert Wuthnow observes:

> All too often, the character of the poor is diminished implicitly in efforts to account for their situation in the first place. They symbolize the opposite of character traits thought to be the basis of middle-class success and security. The poor are thus credited . . . with limited intelligence, an inability to plan, having made bad choices, falling in with bad friends or marrying irresponsible partners, being weak-willed with respect to drugs and alcohol, or simply being lazy.[3]

Yet our living faith says otherwise.[4] For heirs of the biblical promise, the mark of covenant fidelity remains the welfare of the poor—the widow, orphan, and stranger (migrant) in our midst.[5] We face an enduring scandal of poverty: the 736 million (1 in 10) people in extreme poverty, living on less than $1.90 a day; the 822 million chronically undernourished; the two billion suffering from "hidden hunger" due to vitamin and mineral (micronutrient) deficiencies.[6] And as we saw in the previous chapter, property and wealth bear a "social mortgage." In Pope Francis's words,

> Poverty has a face! It has the face of a child; it has the face of a family; it has the face of people, young and old. It has the face of widespread unemployment and lack of opportunity. It has the face of forced migrations, and of empty or destroyed homes.[7]

And the face beckons. An integral framework of basic human rights and correlative duties, as we saw, underwrites our option for the poor or systemically vulnerable. Our moral entitlement to equal respect or consideration (dignity-in-solidarity) justifies preferential treatment for those whose basic rights are most imperiled. The privilege of the poor rests not, then, in the restrictive attribution of rights, but in the moral exigency of their universal claims. Whose equal rights, we must continue to ask, are unequally threatened by systemic deprivation (social sin)? And foremost among such rights is what Henry Shue terms "effective participation," that is, exercising "genuine influence upon the fundamental choices among the social institutions and the social policies."[8]

The poor or systemically vulnerable thus enjoy a privileged role in the design and implementation of social policies affecting their vital interests. Acknowledging this role emerges as a touchstone of the legitimacy of our prevailing institutional arrangements; only thus can we offer an equitable assessment of our laws, juridical decisions, and economic policies. An integral and comprehensive account of basic rights, moreover, underscores the complex interdependence of factors contributing to systemic deprivation. For life's natural lottery[9] is rigged against victims of racial, ethnic, and gender bias:[10]

Women aged between 25 and 34 are 25 percent more likely than men to live in extreme poverty. . . . Improved education among women has done little to shift deeply entrenched occupational segregation in developed and developing countries. . . . Women continue to carry out a disproportionate share of unpaid care and domestic work. . . . Women remain significantly under-represented in or locked out of decision-making and leadership roles across all sectors. . . . Violence against women and girls remains pervasive.[11]

Intrastate ethnic conflict and ethnic cleansing exacerbate the incidence of poverty, hunger, and forced displacement, and the legacy of white privilege persists in South Africa and the United States.[12] Economist and philosopher Amartya Sen writes:

> It is remarkable that the extent of deprivation for par-ticular groups in very rich countries can be comparable to that in the so-called third world. For example, in the United States, African Americans as a group have no higher, indeed have a lower, chance of reaching advanced ages than do people born in the immensely poorer economies of China or the Indian state of Kerala (or in Sri Lanka, Jamaica or Costa Rica. . . . So it is not only the case that American blacks suffer from *rela-tive* deprivation in terms of income per head vis-a-vis American whites, they also are *absolutely* more deprived than the low-income Indians in Kerala (for both women and men), and Chinese (in the case of men), in terms of living to ripe old ages.[13]

Now, as we argued, the option for the poor demands not only denunciation of social sin, but also annunciation of viable alternatives—distributive and social justice require both systemic and specific redress. We must seek policies, programs, and laws that best protect and preserve the basic rights of the most vulnerable, and in particular, their rights to effective participation and representation. Taking the victims' side implies redressing the systemic inequities suffered, including the structural violence of racial, ethnic, and gender discrimination. What Gustavo Gutiérrez terms "the irruption of the poor in history" reveals the "partiality and partisan" nature, not of their claims, but of the prevailing social arrangements that would condemn them, in Óscar Romero's words, to passive "resignation and inactivity."[14]

Effective strategies of poverty reduction must themselves, then, be integral and comprehensive: interdependent basic rights and correlative duties must be fittingly satisfied in a comprehensive rights regime, redressing the interlocking systems of oppression. As we saw in Chapter 7, systemic redress demands the ethical integration of markets, where integral humanism takes priority over the superdevelopment of the privileged. Education of the female child, for instance, is not only morally exigent but serves to secure her health and material well-being, enhancing her effective participation in the political and economic spheres, which in turn promotes greater security. And specific redress demands restitution and reparation for victims of racial, ethnic, and gender bias, such as victims of trafficking or mass incarceration. In Pope Francis's words:

> The fight against poverty demands a better understanding of the reality of poverty as a human and not merely

economic phenomenon. Promoting integral human development demands dialogue and engagement with people's needs and aspirations, listening to the poor and their daily experience of "multidimensional, overlapping deprivations," and devising specific responses to concrete situations. This calls for the creation, within communities and between communities and business, of mediating structures capable of bringing people and resources together, initiating processes in which the poor are the principal actors and beneficiaries.[15]

Questions for Reflection

1. To repeat Robert Wuthnow's quotation from the text above: "All too often, the character of the poor is diminished implicitly in efforts to account for their situation in the first place. They symbolize the opposite of character traits thought to be the basis of middle-class success and security."[16] To what degree is such implicit bias reflected in modern welfare policy? How would you respond to Wuthnow's comment?

2. Pope Francis was quoted above as well: "Promoting integral human development demands dialogue and engagement with people's needs and aspirations, listening to the poor and their daily experience of 'multidimensional, overlapping deprivations,' and devising specific responses to concrete situations."[17] How do "multidimensional, overlapping deprivations," such as those due to race, ethnicity, gender, disability, and orientation, contribute to poverty? What would it mean

to redress such "multidimensional, overlapping deprivations" in our own ministries, such as in community organizing?

   3. Consider the objection that the option for the poor is just that—an option for the exercise of charity voluntarily undertaken by citizens of faith. And charity, as the moral philosophers say, is supererogatory (beyond what justice requires). How would you, then, respond to Emerson's assertion that citizens have no "obligation to put all poor men in good situations"[18]?

Notes

  [1] Robert Bolt, *A Man for All Seasons* (New York: Random House, 1990), 19.

  [2] Ralph Waldo Emerson, "The Essay on Self-Reliance" (East Aurora, NY: Roycrofters, 1908), 14. The full citation reads: "Then, again, do not tell me, as a good man did to-day, of my obligation to put all poor men in good situations. Are they my poor? I tell thee, thou foolish philanthropist, that I grudge the dollar, the dime, the cent, I give to such men as do not belong to me and to whom I do not belong."

  [3] Robert Wuthnow, *God and Mammon in America* (New York: Free Press, 1994), 216.

  [4] See *Compendium of the Social Doctrine of the Church,* nos. 182, 295, 323–76, 433, 447–50.

  [5] Katherine Schaeffer of the Pew Research Center reports: "Income inequality in the U.S. is the highest of all the G7 nations, according to data from the Organization for Economic Cooperation and Development. . . . The wealth gap between America's richest and poorer families more than doubled from 1989 to 2016… The richest families are also the only ones whose wealth increased in the years after the start of the Great Recession." Pew Research Center, "6 facts about economic inequality in the US" (The OECD uses the Gini coefficient in comparing income inequality across countries.) (February 7, 2020).

  [6] Bread for the World data: "Facts on International Poverty and Hunger," http://files.bread.org/campaigns/2020/offering-of-letters-facts-

on-international-hunger-and-poverty.pdf; Hunger Report 2020, "Better Nutrition, Better Tomorrow," https://hungerreport.org/2020/.

[7] Pope Francis, speech at the headquarters of the World Food Program, Rome, June 13, 2016.

[8] Henry Shue, *Basic Rights: Subsistence, Affluence, and US Foreign Policy*, 2nd ed. (Princeton, NJ: Princeton University Press, 1996), 71.

[9] It is actually both a natural and a social lottery. See John Rawls, *A Theory of Justice* (Cambridge, MA: Harvard University Press, 1971), 74, 75.

[10] See Pope Francis, *Fratelli tutti*, nos. 23–24. For Catholic, feminist appropriations of the tradition, see Margaret A. Farley, *Just Love: A Framework for Christian Sexual Ethics* (New York: Continuum, 2006); and Lisa Sowle Cahill, *Global Justice, Christology, and Christian Ethics*, New Studies in Christian Ethics, ed. Robin Gill (New York: Cambridge University Press, 2013).

[11] UN Economic and Social Council, "Review and Appraisal of the Implementation of the Beijing Declaration and Platform for Action and the Outcomes of the Twenty-Third Special Session of the General Assembly: Report of the Secretary-General," Commission on the Status of Women, December 13, 2019, nos. 7–8. See also Susan Moller Okin, "Gender Inequality and Cultural Differences," *Political Theory,* 22, no. 1 (February 1994). Okin concludes, "So long as we are careful, and develop our judgements in the light of empirical evidence, it is possible to generalize about many aspects of inequality between the sexes. From place to place, from class to class, from race to race, and from culture to culture, we find similarities in the specifics of these inequalities, in their causes and effects, although often not in their extent or their severity" (20–21).

[12] See Pope Francis, *Fratelli tutti*, nos. 20, 97. For critical assessments of racism in the Catholic Church and the church's response, see Bryan Massingale, *Racial Justice and the Catholic Church* (Maryknoll, NY: Orbis Books, 2010); and M. Shawn Copeland, *Enfleshing Freedom: Body, Race, and Being* (Minneapolis, MN: Fortress Press, 2010),

[13] Amartya Sen, *Development as Freedom* (New York: Anchor Books, 1999), 21–22.

[14] Gustavo Gutiérrez, *The Truth Shall Make You Free: Confrontations* (Maryknoll, NY: Orbis Books, 1990), 8ff.; Archbishop Óscar Romero, "The Political Dimension of the Faith from the Perspective of the Option for the Poor," in *Liberation Theology: A Documentary History,* ed. Alfred T. Hennelly (Maryknoll, NY: Orbis Books, 1990), 299.

[15] Pope Francis, "Address of His Holiness Pope Francis to the Congress Organized by the *Centesimus Annus*—Pro Pontifice Foundation," May 20, 2017.

[16] Wuthnow, *God and Mammon in America*, 216.

[17] Pope Francis, "Address of His Holiness Pope Francis to the Congress Organized by the *Centesimus Annus*—Pro Pontifice Foundation."

[18] Emerson, "The Essay on Self-Reliance."

9

War and Peace

The great sixteenth-century British physician Thomas Linacre, it is said, first opened the New Testament only late in life. Chancing upon the hard sayings of Matthew's Sermon on the Mount (for example, "turning the other cheek" in 5:39), he was horrified. "Either this is not the Gospel," he exclaimed, "or we are not Christians." Linacre, his biographer tells us, "flung the book from him, and resumed his medical studies."[1]

Even if apocryphal, the story bears a grain of truth. For then, as now, the "things that make for peace," as Dorothy Day once said, seem to slip through the fingers, leaving little room for Matthew's challenging precepts.[2] In a world of uncivil war and the structural violence of racism, gender bias, and poverty, living the "gospel of peace" (Eph 6:15) remains a hard grace.[3] Yet here, too, the church's teaching offers wisdom.[4] Early Christians adopted an evangelical pacifism; it was only after Constantine that Christian theologians like Ambrose and Augustine allowed for the possibility of a just war. Appealing to their Greco-Roman heritage and the tradition of divinely mandated war in the Old Testament, Augustine believed that in the fallen state of civil society, Christian love itself may require a limited use of force in the defense of an innocent neighbor. Augustine writes:

> Peace would be the object of your desire. War should be waged only as a necessity and waged only that through it God may deliver us from that necessity and preserve us in peace. For peace is not to be sought in order to kindle war, but war is to be waged in order to obtain peace. Therefore, even in the course of war you should cherish the spirit of a peace maker.[5]

War must be waged under the auspices of legitimately constituted authority and enhance the possibility of enduring peace with a subjugated enemy.

In fidelity to the scriptures, Augustine argues that "the love of enemies admits of no dispensation, but love does not exclude wars of mercy waged by the good."[6] When motivated by love (*caritas*), punishment of unjust aggressors restores the divinely mandated order of justice for our "earthly city."[7] For Augustine, the ideal of Christian pacifism pertains principally to the inner, spiritual domain (the attitude of love) and personal conduct (self-defense entailing death of an aggressor is unjustified, inasmuch as it implies passionate self-assertion). Nonresistance to evil requires "not a bodily action but an inward disposition."[8]

Codified in the Code of Canon Law, Ambrose's and Augustine's early speculations were elaborated in Thomistic natural law and later refined by the Spanish Scholastics. Unlike Augustine, Aquinas permitted personal self-defense, but waging war was justified only by the common civic good. Indeed, in view of the primacy of neighbor love, Aquinas asks "whether it is *always* sinful to wage war."[9] Like Augustine, Aquinas recognizes the force of the divine precept in Matthew 5:39: "Do not resist an evildoer." Yet while the precept "should always be borne in readiness of mind, so that we are ready to obey (it)," nevertheless, "it is necessary sometimes . . . to act otherwise for the common good, or for the good of those with whom he is fighting" (that is, punishing the sinful with "a kindly severity"). "Those who wage war," moreover, "justly aim at peace."[10]

For Aquinas and his successors, then, war demanded a just cause, legitimate authority, and rightful intention. To these *ad bellum* criteria, the Spanish Scholastics Vitoria and Suárez would add norms for the conduct of war (*in bello*): noncombatant immunity and proportionality. By the Renaissance, the just-war criteria appear as we know them today, that is, the *ad bellum* criteria of just cause (comparative justice), legitimate authority, rightful intention, proportionality, reasonable hope of success, and last reasonable resort; and the *in bello* criteria of noncombatant immunity (discrimination) and proportionality.[11] More recently, some theorists likewise speak of *post bellum* criteria of forging and preserving a just peace.[12]

For Christian tradition, then, war was always tragic, subject to strict limits, and warranted, as a last resort, for the sake of the common good—a good extending even to one's enemies. The Thomistic ideal, to be sure, was often betrayed, most notably in the Crusades and Reformation conflicts. But the traditional "godly" wisdom remained a touchstone for assessing the legitimacy of war. Only with the eclipse of the medieval ideal of the common good in early modernity would a new, secular rationale emerge. In his magisterial *De Jure Belli ac Pacis* (1625), Grotius writes that the "manifest and clear" precepts of natural law retain their validity "*etiamsi daremus non esse Deum* (even if we should concede that which cannot be conceded without the utmost wickedness: that there is no God)."[13] For Grotius, the impious premise cannot be conceded; yet for his successors, the speculative hypothesis soon became a thesis.[14] Under the spell of modernity's disenchantment, Grotius's heirs (Samuel Pufendorf, Jean-Jacques Burlamaqui, and Emmerich de Vattel) regard the validity of the just-war norms as independent of the theological tradition that handed them on. A new, secular wisdom takes the stage.

For Augustine and Aquinas, war could be justified only for the common good. In contrast, Thomas Hobbes appeals to the very right that Augustine denied: self-preservation. The state of nature is no longer a peaceable kingdom but a state of war "of all against all," governed by the "Right of Nature" (*jus naturale)* "to use man's power, as he will himself, for the preservation of his own nature."[15] For Hobbes and his modern heirs, the right of self-defense is writ large on the body politic, bequeathing us not only a legacy of political realism in international relations, but a realist reading of just war: governed by weak international law, sovereign states will abide by the laws of nature (norms of the just war) if, and to the degree to which, they promote self-preservation. The exigencies of national sovereignty (for example, "America First!") prevail, and the victims of even a "just" war, such as refugees, are forgotten as collateral damage. In Pope Francis's words,

"No thought is given to hungry children in refugee camps; no thought is given to forced displacements; no thought is given to destroyed homes; no thought is given now to so many destroyed lives."[16]

Against this reductive reading of the tradition, CST joins with other religious traditions in appealing to our natural social harmony (*Ubuntu*).[17] Violence remains tragic; only *in extremis,* when the rights-based common good of the most vulnerable is threatened, can intervention be justified. For national sovereignty is itself necessarily relativized by the ideal of realizing, incrementally, an integral and comprehensive rights regime—a global common good. Developing church teaching, moreover, recognizes principled pacifism as both a personal and social option bearing witness to the gospel of peace.[18]

During his long tenure Pope John Paul II condemned every war; yet, like Augustine, he supported instances of humanitarian intervention, as a last resort, when the fate and welfare of the most vulnerable were imperiled. In *Fratelli tutti*, Pope Francis questions whether a just war *can* be waged today.[19] Modern popes have all denounced the nuclear arms race, and Pope Francis has gone further in condemning the very existence of nuclear weapons as immoral. In his visit to Nagasaki, Japan, in November 2019, Pope Francis stressed that

> peace and international stability are incompatible with attempts to build upon the fear of mutual destruction, or the threat of total annihilation. They can be achieved only on the basis of a global ethic of solidarity and cooperation in the service of a future shaped by

interdependence and shared responsibility in the whole
human family of today and tomorrow.[20]

Decrying the endemic violence that displaces the vulnerable and despoils the earth, Pope Francis reminds us of the
biblical primacy of peace (*shalom*) and the necessity of just
peacemaking:

> May the common good and respect for every person,
> rather than specific interests, be at the center of every
> decision. Let us remember that in war all is lost and in
> peace nothing. Brothers and sisters, never war! Never
> war! I think mostly of the children, of those who are
> deprived of the hope for a dignified life, of a future:
> dead children, wounded children, maimed children,
> orphaned children, children who have the remnants of
> war as toys, children who do not know how to smile.
> Stop, please! I ask you with all my heart. It is time to
> stop![21]

Questions for Reflection

1. Is it always sinful to wage war? In your experience,
can violence ever be justified? Consider first the case of self-
defense; then consider the case of defending others against
aggression.

2. The just-war norms in Christian tradition (*ad bellum*
and *in bello*) were intended to limit violence in the name of
the common good, including that of one's enemy. Yet many

contemporary secular advocates justify war in the name of self-defense (national security). What difference does the Christian interpretation make? What are its implications today?

3. Some theorists distinguish humanitarian intervention from just war, viewing such intervention as more akin to "just policing." Do you agree? Could a pacifist accept humanitarian intervention, for example, on the analogy of just policing?

Notes

[1] R. W. Chambers, *Thomas More* (Maryland: Westminster Press, 1949), 84.

[2] Dorothy Day, *The Selected Writings of Dorothy Day*, ed. Robert Ellsberg (New York: Alfred A. Knopf, 1988), 280. Day writes: "So many in these days have taken violent steps to gain the things of this world—war to achieve peace; coercion to achieve freedom; striving to gain what slips through the fingers. We might as well give up our great desires, at least our hopes of doing great things toward achieving them, right at the beginning. In a way it is like the paradox of the Gospel, of giving up one's life in order to save it" (September 1957).

[3] Dr. Martin Luther King Jr. condemns the systemic or structural violence of racism in "Letter from Birmingham City Jail," in *A Testament of Hope: The Essential Writings of Martin Luther King, Jr.,* ed. James Melvin Washington (San Francisco: Harper and Row, 1986), 289–302.

[4] See *Compendium of the Church's Social Doctrine*, nos. 488–520.

[5] Augustine, Letter 189, "Letter to Boniface," trans. J. G. Cunningham, in *Nicene and Post-Nicene Fathers, First Series*, vol. 1, ed. Philip Schaff (Buffalo, NY: Christian Literature Publishing Co., 1887), par. 6.

[6] Augustine, *Sermo Dom.* I, xx, 63 and 70; Epist. 138, ii, 14. (In *Retractationes* I, xix, 1.) Cited in Roland Bainton, *Christian Attitudes toward War and Peace: A Historical Survey and Critical Re-evaluation* (Nashville, TN: Abingdon, 1960), 91–93.

[7] Augustine, Letter 138, "Letter to Marcellinus," in Schaff, *Nicene and Post-Nicene Fathers, First Series*, vol. 1.

[8] Augustine, "Reply to Faustus the Manichaean," trans. Richard Stothert (Buffalo, NY: Christian Publishing Co., 1886), par. 76.

[9] Thomas Aquinas, *Summa Theologiae* II–II, Q. 40 (emphasis added).

[10] Ibid.

[11] See US Bishops, *The Challenge of Peace: God's Promise and Our Response*," pars. 85–100. Cf. *Catechism of the Catholic Church*, nos. 2309–13; *Compendium of the Church's Social Doctrine*, nos. 500–13. In some accounts satisfying the *ad bellum* norms likewise implies a formal declaration by competent authority.

[12] See Michael Schuck, "When the Shooting Stops: Missing Elements in Just War Theory," *The Christian Century* 101 (October 26, 1999): 982–84; Brian Orend, "Justice after War," *Ethics and International Affairs* 16 (2002): 43–56.

[13] Hugo Grotius, "Prologue," *On the Law of War and Peace,* ed. Stephen C. Neff (Cambridge: Cambridge University Press, 2012), 4.

[14] See Alexander Passerin d' Entrèves, *Natural Law: An Introduction to Legal Philosophy* (New York: Routledge, 1994), 37–50.

[15] Thomas Hobbes, *Leviathan,* in *British Moralists: 1650–1800,* ed. D. D. Raphael, vol. 1 (Oxford: Clarendon Press, 1969), 11:32, 36 and 14:38–39.

[16] Pope Francis, "Address to Participants in the World Meeting of Popular Movements," October 28, 2014.

[17] See Chapter 2 of this volume.

[18] Similar considerations arise with respect to capital punishment. Doctrine has developed with "increasing awareness that the dignity of the person is not lost after the commission of very serious crimes." So too, "a new understanding has emerged of the significance of penal sanctions imposed by the state. Lastly, more effective systems of detention have been developed, which ensure the due protection of citizens but, at the same time, do not definitively deprive the guilty of the possibility of redemption." Initially revised under Pope John Paul II, the *Catechism of the Catholic Church* now reflects Pope Francis's spirituality of nonviolence: "Consequently, the Church teaches, in the light of the Gospel, that 'the death penalty is inadmissible because it is an attack on the inviolability and dignity of the person', and she works with determination for its abolition worldwide" ("New Revision of Number 2267 of the Catechism of the Catholic Church on the Death Penalty," *Rescriptum ex "Ex Audientia SS.Mi"*; see Pope Francis, *Fratelli tutti*, nos. 263–70.)

[19] Pope Francis, *Fratelli tuti*, nos. 256–62. Appealing to the criterion of proportionality, Pope Francis argues: "We can no longer think of war as a solution, because its risks will probably always be greater than its supposed benefits. In view of this, it is very difficult nowadays to invoke the rational criteria elaborated in earlier centuries to speak of the possibility of a 'just war'" (no. 258).

[20] Pope Francis, "Address of the Holy Father on Nuclear Weapons," Atomic Bomb Hypocenter Park, Nagasaki, Japan, November 24, 2019.

[21] Pope Francis, "Angelus," July 27, 2014.

10

Just Peacemaking

War, says Michael Walzer, is a "rule-governed activity, a world of permissions and prohibitions—a moral world," even "in the midst of hell."[1] Yet which rules? For some contemporary theorists, the *ad bellum* and *in bello* norms of just war represent reasoned exceptions to a general rule or duty of nonviolence. For others, conversely, such an interpretation defers excessively to the Christian pacifist tradition. The just-war tradition begins, they say, not with peace (nonviolence), but rather with the duty of justice.[2]

As we argued in the Introduction, however, CST, like the scriptures that inspire it, cannot be reduced to a set of rules. The tradition is, rather, a living word, a wisdom, and a way of life where key themes or motifs cohere like the grammar of a language. For CST, then, justice and peace are not opposed. In the Psalmist's words, "righteousness [justice] and peace will kiss each other" (Ps 85:10). For peace is never "simply the absence of conflict."[3] Rather, writes Pope Francis, citing his predecessor Pope Paul VI, "it is fashioned by efforts directed day after day towards the establishment of the ordered universe willed by God, with a more perfect justice among all."[4]

For the tradition, genuine peace can never be unjust; nor can it mask the systemic violence of racism, ethnic bias, and so on, "which silences or appeases the poor."[5] A harvest of righteousness is sown in peace for those who make peace" (Jas 3:18). Just as peace presumes justice, so justice implies peacemaking. For dignity, we saw in Chapter 2, binds us in solidarity, the social harmony deriving from our divine creation and redemption. Our natural state, though marred by sin, both personal and social, never ceases to be *shalom* (peace). For the living tradition, as we saw in the previous chapter, is that violence always remains tragic. It is always, in Pope Francis's words, "a defeat for humanity."[6] Yet wisdom demands discernment. For neither Christian pacifists nor advocates of humanitarian intervention does scripture or tradition provide a simple action guide determining conduct.

Both, we argued, are bound by a nonviolent way of life, the living faith of our ancestors. Neither can accept Thomas Hobbes's brute economy of violence. And so, in mediating the tradition, we must seek to restore the common good by opting for the poor, asking (1) Who will suffer most from war and ethnic conflict (including innocent victims)? (2) What are the best means of general redress of violence and the structures of sin abetting violence? and (3) What are the best means of specific redress of victims? How we answer these questions will reveal differing strains of a common tradition. Some may follow Pope John Paul II in recognizing the limit case of humanitarian intervention when the lives and livelihood of the most vulnerable are threatened. Others, conversely, contend that no violence can ever stem the cycle of violence or help us "pursue what makes for peace" (Rom 14:19).

Pacifist and interventionist alike are bound by the "grammar" of the tradition; neither can neglect the demands of the common good, that is, of general and specific redress. In terms of their Christian inspiration, then, both bear a family resemblance, though differences remain. But to an even greater degree, both differ from the dominant, secular interpretation of just war—one, as we have seen, more beholden to Hobbes (and Machiavelli) than to the kindly harshness of Augustine and Aquinas. Pope Francis has repeatedly deplored the violence of Machiavelli's armed prophets in his advocacy of just peacemaking and nonviolent strategies of conflict resolution. For Pope Francis, "Peacebuilding through active nonviolence is the natural and necessary complement to the Church's continuing efforts to limit the use of force by the application of moral norms; she does so by her participation in the work of international institutions and through the competent contribution made by so many Christians to the drafting of legislation at all levels."[7]

Both pacifist and inteventinonist must walk in the way of peace (Lk 1:79), denouncing arms profiteering, nuclear armament, state repression, terrorism, and so on. Still, the question remains: Is recourse to violence *ever* justified in defending the innocent neighbor? Here, we hark back to the very origins of Christian reflection on just war, for not all were ordained to fight.[8] In Ambrose's words, "It was not the clergy's business to look to arms but rather to the forces of peace."[9] And Augustine counsels Boniface that "they occupy indeed a higher place before God who, abandoning all these secular employments, serve Him with the strictest chastity, but 'every one,' as the apostle says, 'hath his proper gift of God, one after this manner, and another after that' (1 Corinthians 7:7).[10] For Aquinas, too, the "higher" calling of clergy and religious precludes resort to lethal force.[11]

With the Second Vatican Council's universal call to holiness, such distinctions of higher or lesser meritorious roles no longer obtain. Neither does appeal to legitimate authority justify citizen soldiers' obedience to what Augustine called "unjust commands" of "temporal masters."[12] In the way of discipleship no one is spared the hard grace of discernment. We return, then, to our initial discussion of discernment in Chapter 6, where Karl Rahner distinguishes essential and formal existential ethics, figuring respectively in the first and second week of Saint Ignatius's *Spiritual Exercises.* In Rahner's spirituality, essential ethics defines the sphere of *universal* norms, while a formal existential ethics pertains to discerning the *particular* call of God to the disciple, one's ownmost self, "whom God has called by name, a name which is and can only be unique."[13] Moral deliberation brings us to the brink of such discernment, but in the formal existential ethics of the second week's election, we are summoned by name to respond to God's gracious invitation. For Rahner, not all moral decisions are mapped onto practical syllogisms; rather, God graciously invites each to a particular state, one not morally superior to another.

Since Vatican II, Catholic teaching has increasingly recognized the role of the pacifist's *vocation* in the church. Might we then treat pacifism or humanitarian intervention not as a question of "essentialist" moral inference but rather of graced discernment? If so, I may fully trust in my vocation yet not be compelled to condemn yours. And if we need not condemn, then perhaps we may learn each from the other: pacifists reminding interventionists of their original inspiration, the gospel of peace; and interventionists recalling our common duty to seek effective means of general and specific redress for the most vulnerable victims of violence.[14] May we witness rather than judge in healing our breaches? For, as Pope Francis reminds us, in living Luke's parable of the good Samaritan:

Jesus does not make us cross to the other side alone; instead, he asks us to make the crossing with him, as each of us responds to his or her own specific vocation. We need to realize that making this crossing can only be done with him, by freeing ourselves of divisive notions of family and blood in order to build a Church which is God's family, open to everyone, concerned for those most in need. This presupposes closeness to our brothers and sisters; it implies a spirit of communion.[15]

Questions for Reflection

1. Can the differences between Christian pacifists and advocates of humanitarian intervention be reconciled? If so,

how? What might the pacifist learn from the interventionist, and what might the interventionist learn from the pacifist?

2.   We read above that Pope Francis has declared that "peacebuilding through active nonviolence is the natural and necessary complement to the Church's continuing efforts to limit the use of force by the application of moral norms."[16] Why does the pope advocate active nonviolence in just peacemaking? What are the fruits of nonviolent witness today?

3.   Violence often begets violence in a vicious cycle. What means of nonviolent resistance, religious or secular, can interrupt such cycles of violence?

Notes

[1] Michael Walzer, *Just and Unjust Wars: A Moral Argument with Historical Illustrations,* 3rd ed. (New York: Basic Books, 1977), 36.

[2] For an assessment of conflicting interpretations, see William O'Neill, "'Must the Violent Bear It Away?' A Restorative Critique of Just War," *Ethics in Focus* 12, no. 1 (2018): 103–25.

[3] John R. Donahue, SJ, "What Does the Lord Require? A Bibliographical Essay on the Bible and Social Justice," *Studies in the Spirituality of Jesuits* 25, no. 2 (1993), 70.

[4] Pope Francis, *Evangelii gaudium*, no. 219, citing Pope Paul VI, *Populorum progressio,* no. 76.

[5] *Evangelii gaudium,* no. 218.

[6] Pope Francis, "Vigil of Prayer for Peace," September 7, 2013. Cf. Pope John Paul II, "Address of His Holiness Pope John Paul II to the Diplomatic Corps," January 13, 2003; Pope Paul VI, "Address of His Holiness Pope Paul VI to the United Nations Organization," October 4, 1965.

[7] Pope Francis, "Message for the World Day of Peace," December 8, 2016.

[8] Roland Bainton, *Christian Attitudes toward War and Peace: A Historical Survey and Critical Re-evaluation* (Nashville, TN: Abingdon, 1960), 89. For an excellent account of the church's contemporary teaching, see Lisa Sowle

Cahill, *Blessed Are the Peacemakers: Pacifism, Just War, and Peacebuilding* (Minneapolis, MN: Fortress Press, 2019).

⁹ Ambrose, "On the Duties of the Clergy," trans. H. De Romestin, with the assistance of E. De Romestin and H.T.F. Duckworth (New York: Christian Literature Publishing Co., 1886), Bk. 1, Chapter XXXV, par. 175.

¹⁰ Augustine, Letter 189, "Letter to Boniface," in *Nicene and Post-Nicene Fathers,* vol. 1, *The Confessions and Letters of Augustine, with a Sketch of His Life and Word, First Series,* ed. Philip Schaff, trans. J. G. Cunningham, 552–54 (Peabody, MA: Hendrickson Publishers, 1994), 553.

¹¹ Aquinas, *ST* II-II, Q. 40, a. 2: "Although it is meritorious to wage a just war, nevertheless it is rendered unlawful for clerics, by reason of their being deputed to works more meritorious still"; cf. II-II, Q. 64, a. 4.

¹² Augustine, Commentary on Psalm 125, in *Expositions on the Books of Psalms,* vol. 5, trans. H. M. Wilkins, vol. 37 in *A Library of the Fathers of the Holy Catholic Church* (London: F and J Rivington, 1835), 543.

¹³ Karl Rahner, "On the Question of a Formal Existential Ethics," in *Theological Investigations* 2, trans. Karl H. Kruger (Baltimore: Helicon, 1963), 217–34.

¹⁴ A formal-existential ethics of discipleship, as we saw in Chapter 6, draws upon differing spiritualities; here I have considered only the implications of Ignatian spirituality. As we noted at the beginning of this chapter, differences between pacifists and those appealing to just-war norms (for example, in humanitarian intervention) remain, and for some are irreconcilable.

¹⁵ Pope Francis, "Meeting with Authorities and the Diplomatic Corps, Visit to Kenya," November 25, 2015.

¹⁶ Pope Francis, "Message for the World Day of Peace."

11

What We Owe Forced Migrants and Refugees

In living the tradition we must pass over to or draw near to the suffering of our world.[1] As for the biblical prophets the touchstone of covenant fidelity was the well-being of the widow, orphan, and migrant, so our faith in dignity and human rights will be shown in our response to the most vulnerable in our midst.[2] Lamenting the deaths of migrants at Lampedusa, Italy, Pope Francis recalls God's words to Cain in Genesis:

> God is asking each of us: "Where is the blood of your brother which cries out to me?" Today no one in our world feels responsible; we have lost a sense of responsibility for our brothers and sisters. We have fallen into the hypocrisy of the priest and the Levite whom Jesus described in the parable of the Good Samaritan: we see our brother half dead on the side of the road, and perhaps we say to ourselves: "Poor soul . . . !", and then go on our way. It's not our responsibility, and with that we

feel reassured, assuaged. . . . In this globalized world, we have fallen into globalized indifference.[3]

As we noted in Chapter 5, in passing over to the side of the forcibly displaced, the tradition bids us ask these questions: Whose equal dignity and basic rights are unequally threatened or denied by systemic deprivation? What are the best means of general redress, that is, of securing the basic rights of the forcibly displaced? What are the best means of specific redress, that is, of securing their special rights, for example, to asylum? These three distinct yet related questions reveal the place of displacement in an ethics of integral humanism, one only imperfectly enshrined in national law and international conventions. Let us briefly consider each question.

Whose Equal Rights Are Most Threatened?

Albert Camus writes that life is not tragic merely because it is wretched.[4] To many in our world today, the suffering of forced migrants is no more than an unimportant failure of global politics. Faced with the reality of statelessness, we see, as Pope Francis says, but pass by.[5] Like the nameless, half-dead stranger in Luke's parable, our world, in Hannah Arendt's words, finds "nothing sacred in the abstract nakedness of being human." Indeed, writes Arendt, our very "right to have rights" typically depends upon membership in a particular national, ethnic, racial, or religious community, so that the "loss of home and political status" is tantamount to "expulsion from humanity altogether."[6] The alien becomes not the exemplar of humanity, but "a frightening symbol of difference as such."[7] Is it surprising, then, that we speak of illegal aliens—those whose very bodies, rather than their behavior, become illegal?

This first question reveals the critical role of rights in CST in letting us imagine otherwise—letting us *see* forcible displacement as a betrayal of the human community present in each. Dignity is realized in solidarity, in *belonging* to a moral community; to be forcibly displaced, to be denied one's place in the world, is to be effaced, divested of legal and even moral standing. The crisis of refugees is finally a crisis of human rights, the very name *refugee* signifying systemic rights deprivation. And yet, the crisis of rights extends beyond such official, legal recognition.

Internally displaced persons (IDPs), stateless persons, migrants fleeing famine, generalized violence, or systemic deprivation—though excluded in varying degrees from the strict formal protections afforded refugees under the Geneva accords—are victims of rights violations.[8] Neither do the criteria stipulated in the 1951 Refugee Convention reflect the gender-specific persecution that women and girl children endure, such as rape, genital mutilation, domestic abuse, and forced marriages, or the particular vulnerabilities of LGBTQ+ persons.

Best Means of General Redress

Basic rights, we saw in Chapter 3, impose correlative duties of both forbearance and performance (protection and provision). And duties migrate before persons do. Where intrastate protections fail, leading to forced displacement, duties correlative to basic human rights persist, falling now upon the community of states. The concrete *universality* of citizenship in guaranteeing human *rights* binds us in a family of solidarities, privileging those most vulnerable. An integral rights regime, then, would address the complex "push" factors of forced migration—not only the well-founded fear of persecution, but generalized violence, famine, disease, and environmental degradation. Rights and duties hang together; thus, to threaten any basic human right imperils all. The systemic violation of security rights underlying forced migration threatens subsistence and curtails liberty. But so too, systemic deprivation of adequate nutrition, healthcare, education, and so on, impels families to migrate.

Basic rights are further threatened as those forced to migrate face violence, sexual assault, and insecurity—perils exacerbated as receiving countries seek to "deter" asylum-seekers by closing borders. The litany of deaths lamented by Pope Francis extends from Lampedusa to the southwest deserts of the United States. Refugees and IDPs, especially those in protracted refugee situations, are often systematically deprived of basic subsistence rights. Denying rights to adequate nutrition, potable water, education, and healthcare, or making their attainment dependent upon charity, threatens both refugees' security and civil liberty. Seeking firewood for survival, often at considerable distances, women in refugee camps are put at risk of rape or other forms of gender and sexually based violence. This vulnerability is only exacerbated by a denial of their civil-political rights to participate effectively in the design and implementation of policies affecting them and their dependents in the camps.[9]

In a world ever more interdependent, citizens must seek a continual revision of programs, systems, and regimes so as to guarantee the full and effective implementation of the rights of the most vulnerable, including those condemned to stateless existence in camps of first asylum (particularly women and children). Such guarantees, as we argued above, must provide effective legal-juridical redress of gender-specific forms of violence, including rape and genital mutilation. And because duties are a function of relative capability,[10] wealthier states must bear a fair share of the burden disproportionately borne by the poorer countries of first asylum.[11]

Best Means of Specific Redress

Refugees' "right to have rights" must be secured through systemic general redress of our international refugee regime. But we must also address the consequences of denying such rights. The forcibly displaced, that is, claim *specific* rights of redress just because they are forcibly displaced. Foremost among such rights in international refugee law, although restricted to those formally designated refugees or asylees, is that of *non-refoulement,* which means that refugees or asylees cannot be forcibly repatriated to a country where there is a reasonable expectation of persecution.[12] The Universal Declaration of Human Rights acknowledges that refugees have the right to seek and to enjoy asylum. Yet neither the 1951 Refugee Convention nor the 1967 Protocol imposes a correlative obligation upon states to grant it. Indeed, as primary respondents of basic claim-rights, states often summarily dismiss asylum claims, even though *non-refoulement* remains a non-derogative right (a right that cannot be curtailed).

Interdiction in international waters, extraterritorial processing, and indefinite detention further erode potential asylees' basic security. As we argued above, moreover, an integral and comprehensive rights regime would likewise extend the refugee regime to encompass victims of generalized violence or famine. Indeed, the graduated urgency of basic rights and correlative duties serves to indicate the lineaments of an equitable policy of specific redress: where, morally, borders remain porous, international and domestic law should take due cognizance of the moral priority of relative need (the gravity and imminence of harm); particular vulnerabilities of women and children; familial relationships; complicity of the host country in generating refugee flows; historical or cultural affiliations such as historic patterns of migration; and, as we argued above, a fair distribution of burdens among countries offering asylum.[13] The last consideration applies domestically as well, for the burdens of local integration or resettlement should not fall disproportionately upon the most vulnerable citizens. Indeed, where humanitarian "charitable" assistance may pit refugee against host community or engender dependency, an integral and comprehensive account of rights locates refugees' claims within the systemic imperatives of equitable development and regional security.[14]

Even the granting of asylum is no guarantee of basic rights:

In many situations refugees are barred from engaging in political activities. . . . They often lack a clearly defined legal status, do not have long-term resident rights and have no prospect of seeking naturalization in their country of asylum. . . . A further right denied to many refugees is the ability to engage in agricultural, wage-earning and income-generating opportunities. They do not have access to land, they are not allowed to enter the labour market, they cannot take out loans, and restrictions on their freedom of movement make it difficult for them to engage in trade.[15]

And, as we noted above, with the loss of traditional means of protection, women and children in camps, especially those who are unaccompanied, remain vulnerable to exploitation in the form of domestic abuse, rape, sexual exploitation, and so on.[16] Forfeiting even limited legal protection in the camps, urban refugees similarly suffer discrimination in education, housing, employment, access to financial services, and other matters.[17]

Finally, consistent with CST, an integral and comprehensive rights regime would entail equitable policies of voluntary repatriation, reintegration, rehabilitation, and reconstruction (with particular attention to legal rights of widows and unaccompanied women and children); hospitable treatment of those seeking to change nationality, whether through local integration in the host country or resettlement in a third country; assistance in integration into a new homeland;

respect for their cultural heritage; and recognition of the benefits of hosting, and the contribution of, migrants. Above all, there is no "place" for warehousing refugees or incarcerating those seeking asylum, the criminalization of displacement. As for the prophets long ago, the well-being of migrants will be a mark of legitimacy, and hence of citizenship—a state's democratic self-constitution warranted precisely inasmuch as rights render its borders porous.[18]

Pope Paul VI in 1971 urged acceptance of "a charter which will assure them [emigrants] a right to emigrate, favor their integration, facilitate their professional advancement and give them access to decent housing where, if such is the case, their families can join them."[19] As we saw above, in accordance with the principle of subsidiarity, among the most pressing duties in such a charter would be the preservation and protection of families, and of these the most vulnerable, for example, victims of trafficking. In his message for the 104th World Day of Migrants and Refugees, Pope Francis called for a solidarity that

> must be concretely expressed at every stage of the migratory experience—from departure through journey to arrival and return. This is a great responsibility which the Church intends to share with all believers and men and women of good will, who are called to respond to the many challenges of contemporary migration with generosity, promptness, wisdom and foresight, each according to their own abilities.[20]

Questions for Reflection

1.   What human rights claims are embodied in the stories of refugees or forced migrants? In your experience, are these stories heard, and if not, why not?

2.   What rights and duties are particularly relevant to those refugees or forced migrants whom you have come to know? Which of these rights are protected in international and national law, and which rights should be guaranteed in accordance with CST?

3.   How are the basic rights of forced migrants interconnected? For example, how do rights of effective participation for women (having their voices heard) affect the protection of others' rights-claims, such as adequate nutrition or security for their families?

Notes

[1] The United Nations High Commissioner for Refugees (UNHCR) reports on its website that current levels of displacement are the highest ever recorded. An unprecedented 79.5 million people have been forced from their homes, including nearly 26.0 million refugees, approximately 40 percent of whom are under the age of eighteen. At least 45.7 million have been internally displaced (UNHCR, *Global Trends: Forced Displacement in 2019,* June 18, 2020).

[2] See *Compendium of Catholic Social Doctrine*, nos. 297–98, 308, 505.

[3] Pope Francis, "Visit to Lampedusa: Homily of Holy Father Francis," July 8, 2013.

[4] Albert Camus, *Lyrical and Critical Essays*, trans. Ellen Conroy Kennedy (New York: Alfred A. Knopf, 1968), 201.

[5] See Pope Francis, *Fratelli tutti*, nos. 37–41, 56–86, 129–36.

[6] Hannah Arendt, "The Perplexities of the Rights of Man," in *The Origins of Totalitarianism* (New York: Harcourt, Brace and World, 1966), 290, 299.

[7] Ibid., 297, 301.

[8] Refugee law is governed by the Convention Relating to the Status of Refugees (1951) and the Protocol Relating to the Status of Refugees (1967). It includes victims of general insecurity or famine. Definitions that are more inclusive are already accepted by the Organization of African Unity (OAU) Convention Governing the Specific Aspects of Refugee Problems in Africa (1969), the Cartagena Declaration on Refugees (1984) endorsed by the Organization of American States (OAS), and in the operational practice of the UNHCR. See UNHCR, *The State of the World's Refugees: In Search of Solutions* (New York: Oxford University, 1995), esp. "Protecting Human Rights," 57–94.

[9] See Binaifer Nowrojee, "Sexual Violence, Gender Roles, and Displacement" in *Refugee Rights, Ethics Advocacy, and Africa*, ed. David Hollenbach, SJ (Washington, DC: Georgetown University Press, 2008), 125–36; and Susan Martin, "Justice, Women's Rights, and Forced Migration," in Hollenbach, *Refugee Rights, Ethics Advocacy, and Africa*, 137–60.

[10] It is not only, then, that "ought implies can"; it is also that "can implies ought."

[11] Today, 73 percent of refugees and displaced Venezuelans live in neighboring countries. "Developing countries hosted 85 per cent of the world's refugees and Venezuelans displaced abroad. The Least Developed Countries provided asylum to 27 per cent of the total" (UNHCR, *Global Trends: Forced Displacement in 2019,* June 18, 2020).

[12] Other rights enumerated by international convention, yet often overridden or infringed upon, include freedom of religion, education, social security, public assistance, work, and limited travel documents. See Guy S. Goodwin-Gil, *The Refugee in International Law*, 2nd ed. (Oxford: Clarendon, 1966).

[13] See David Hollenbach, *Humanity in Crisis: Ethical and Religious Response to Refugees* (Washington, DC: Georgetown University Press, 2019), 96–113; and, for an incisive application of CST, Kristin Heyer, *Kinship across Borders: A Christian Ethics of Immigration* (Washington, DC: Georgetown University Press, 2012).

[14] See Gil Loescher and James Milner, *Protracted Refugee Situations: Domestic and International Security Implications* (London: International Institute for Strategic Studies, 2005), 67–84.

[15] UNHCR, *The State of the World's Refugees 2006: Human Displacement in the New Millennium* (Oxford: Oxford University Press, 2006), 47.

[16] Loescher and Milner, *Protracted Refugee Situations*, 35–65.

[17] UNHCR, *The State of the World's Refugees 2006,* 50. See Abebe Feyissa's eloquent testimony in "There Is More than One Way of Dying: An Ethiopian Perspective on the Effects of Long-Term Stays in Refugee Camps," with Rebecca Horn, in Hollenbach, *Refugee Rights, Ethics Advocacy, and Africa*, 13–26; and John Burton Wagacha and John Guiney, "The Plight of Urban Refugees in Nairobi, Kenya," in Hollenbach, *Refugee Rights, Ethics Advocacy, and Africa*, 91–102.

[18] See Seyla Benhabib, *The Rights of Others: Aliens, Residents and Citizens* (Cambridge: Cambridge University Press, 2004), 120, 211, 221.

[19] Pope Paul VI, *Octogesima adveniens*, no. 17.

[20] Pope Francis, "Message of His Holiness Pope Francis for the 104th World Day of Migrants and Refugees," January 14, 2018.

12

Hospitality for Migrants

The solidarity Pope Francis speaks of is "small-c Catholic," embracing all people of good will. But it is also "capital-C Catholic," calling believers to practice biblical hospitality. For what is "handed on" (*traditio*) is a *living* Word. Leviticus bids us to remember the stranger or resident alien in our midst:

> When an alien resides with you in your land, you shall not oppress the alien. The alien who resides with you shall be to you as the citizen among you; you shall love the alien as yourself; for you were aliens in the land of Egypt: I am the Lord your God. (19:33–34)[1]

Except for worship of the one God, no command is repeated more often in the Hebrew Bible. In such lived remembrance Israel proves its covenant fidelity in works of justice.[2]

For the children of exile, freedom is always *bonded,* always proven true in the welfare of the poor—the widow, orphan, and migrant.[3] In times of prosperity, Israel is thus summoned to remember that the land "was a gift not a birthright."[4] And so it is in gracious hospitality to the widow, orphan, and stranger—those most vulnerable in kinship societies—that Israel realizes its distinctive covenant identity.[5] To oppress the alien, conversely, is no less than betrayal. Israel must ever cherish the alien, for "you know the heart of an alien, for you were aliens in the land of Egypt" (Ex 23:9). Cultivating the virtue of hospitality to the stranger or alien is thus no mere special act of charity, as hospitality is often seen today.[6] It is the measure of righteousness and justice, the believer's token of belonging.

For Christians, too, memory speaks. In Luke's Gospel, Jesus begins his prophetic ministry by quoting the words of Isaiah,

> "The Spirit of the Lord is upon me,
>   because he has anointed me to bring
>   good news to the poor." (Lk 4:21)

These words are an invitation and demand extended to every disciple. At the heart of Christian ethics is the law of love;[7] for Jesus in Luke's Gospel, it is the stranger, the despised Samaritan, not the scribe or religious expert, who reveals the love commandment's meaning. "Love," writes Wolfgang Schrage, "does not follow the dictates of convention and prejudice but dares to ignore them, dares with sovereign freedom to surmount the barriers that separate people. A person who loves can see in anyone a neighbor in need."[8]

Only in solidarity with the stranger—like the man fallen among thieves, who was stripped of title, status, and role (Lk 10:25–37)—do disciples prove themselves faithful to the covenantal demands of love. The disciple must "see and have compassion" (*esplanchnisthe* signifies being moved in one's inmost heart, not mere pity). Indeed, compassion becomes the disciple's way of seeing the stranger, in Simone Weil's words, as someone "exactly like me," although "stamped with a special mark by affliction."[9] And, as so often in the parables, Jesus turns the table on the questioner. For while the lawyer seeks to set the limits of love by asking who is or is not his neighbor, Jesus speaks the parable and asks, "Which of these three, do you think, was a neighbor to the man who fell into the hands of the robbers?" Then he commands: "Go and do likewise!" For Christians, this means that one must *become* neighbor, "pass over" to the side of the suffering stranger.

In Søren Kierkegaard's words, "Christ does not speak about recognizing one's neighbor but about being a neighbor oneself, about proving oneself to be a neighbor, something the Samaritan showed by his compassion."[10] For Gustavo Gutiérrez, as we noted in Chapter 6, "to be a Christian is to draw near, to make oneself a neighbor, not the one I encounter in my journey but the one in whose journey I place myself."[11] The journey is our story, the gospel in which we "are finally no longer strangers and aliens, but fellow citizens with the saints and also members of the household of God" (Eph 2:19). And this makes all the difference.

Not surprisingly then, Christian hospitality to strangers and aliens is at the very heart of Christian discipleship. In Donald Senior's words, "Jesus begins his earthly journey as a migrant and a displaced person—Jesus who in this same gospel would radically identify with the 'least' and make hospitality to the stranger a criterion of judgment (Mt 25:35)."[12] And for Luke, with saving irony, "seeing and having compassion" for these "least"—for example, the naked, half-dead stranger—marks the way of eternal life. Luke's narrative reveals the boundless, universal scope of love precisely in demanding a moral solidarity with those who suffer. Again and again, in the image of the eschatological feast,[13] hospitality is offered not to kin and kind, but to those whose only claim is vulnerability and need.[14]

For disciples of the way,[15] such displacement becomes the place of revelation. Hebrews recalls the revelatory hospitality of Sarah and Abraham at Mamre in Genesis 18: "Do not neglect to show hospitality to strangers, for by doing that some have entertained angels without knowing it" (Heb 13:2). And in the Synoptic Gospels the image of a feast "for all peoples" (Isa 25:6), reveals God "powerfully and eschatologically as Israel's host"—a fundamental theme recalled in the eschatological memory of the Eucharist. Paul's admonitions to the Corinthian Church "show that issues of justice and concern for the more vulnerable members of the community enter into the most central act of Christian community, the celebration of the Lord's supper."[16]

For disciples, then, the migrant is never the object of a policy of assimilation, but rather a source of blessing. Indeed, both guest and host are transformed as the "alien who resides with you" is treated "as the citizen among you" (Lev 19:34). Like Israel of exile, a church inspired by the parable of the good Samaritan must "become what it has never been before": a "new creation," born of suffering, yes, but more, of resilience, and hope—even hoping against hope.[17] As "strangers and foreigners on earth," Senior notes, Christians seek "a better homeland," the world-affirming reign of God.[18]

For Matthew, as for Luke, such hospitality, transforming guest *and* host, becomes, according to Senior, the very condition of salvation (Mt 25:35).[19] "I was a stranger," unrecognized, "and you welcomed me."[20] In Pope Francis's words, "Every stranger who knocks at our door is an opportunity for an encounter with Jesus Christ, who identifies with the welcomed and rejected strangers of every age (*Matthew* 25:35–43)."[21] In the parable of the final judgment (Mt 25:31–46), the disciple passes over from being host to being the guest of Christ at the eschatological feast. In loving, one comes to see oneself—one is revealed—as beloved. And so grace does what seems to outstrip human possibility: we "pass over" to the crucified *and* risen One—who first "passed over" to us. As Augustine wrote, Christ is our good Samaritan, coming to the aid of our wounded humanity.[22]

Questions for Reflection

1. Hospitality in modern Western culture is often viewed as a charitable act—praiseworthy, but not a matter of justice. In light of the biblical understanding of hospitality, how would you respond?

2. How does the religious imaginary (its stories, images, figures) shape our understanding of forced migration, for example, in how refugees or forced migrants view themselves? What similar stories, images, and figures inform *your* understanding?

3. Forced migrants are often seen as a burden on the host community. Yet, as we saw, in the biblical imagination hosts become guests and guests become hosts. What blessings do migrants bring to the church and to society? What do their stories teach us?

Notes

[1] For a consideration of Israel's sabbath obligation to treat the landless poor as brothers and sisters, see Walter Brueggemann, *The Land*, 2nd ed. (Minneapolis: Fortress Press, 1977), 56–65.

[2] For an interpretation of biblical conceptions of justice, see John Donahue, "The Bible and Catholic Social Teaching: Will This Engagement Lead to Marriage?" in *Modern Catholic Social Teaching: Commentaries and Interpretations*, ed. Kenneth R. Himes, 9–40 (Washington, DC: Georgetown University Press, 2004).

[3] Michael Walzer, *Exodus and Revolution* (New York: Basic Books, 1985), 53, 73–90.

[4] Donald Senior, "Beloved Aliens and Exiles," in *A Promised Land, A Perilous Journey: Theological Perspectives on Migration*, ed. Daniel G. Groody and Gioacchino Campese, 20–34 (Notre Dame, IN: University of Notre Dame Press, 2009), 21.

[5] See John Koenig, "Hospitality," in *The Anchor Bible Dictionary*, vol. 3, ed. David Noel Freedman (New York: Doubleday, 1992), 299–301.

[6] See Christine D. Pohl, *Making Room: Recovering Hospitality as a Christian Tradition* (Grand Rapids, MI: Eerdmans, 1999).

[7] See Lk 10:27; cf. Lev 19:18, 33; Dt 6:4ff.; Mk 12:30–31; Mt 22:37–38.

[8] Wolfgang Schrage, *The Ethics of the New Testament*, trans. David E. Green (Philadelphia: Fortress, 1988), 74, 76.

[9] Simone Weil, "Reflections on the Right Use of School Studies with a View to the Love of God," in Simone Weil, *Waiting for God*, trans. Emma Craufurd, 105–16 (New York: G. P. Putnam's Sons, 1951), 115.

[10] Søren Kierkegaard, *Works of Love,* trans. Howard and Edna Hong (New York: Harper and Row, 1962), 38.

[11] Gustavo Gutiérrez, "Toward a Theology of Liberation" (July 1968), trans. Alfred T. Hennelly, in *Liberation Theology: A Documentary History*, ed. Alfred T. Hennelly, 62–76 (Maryknoll, NY: Orbis Books, 1990), 74.

[12] Senior, "Beloved Aliens and Exiles."

[13] See Am 9:13–15; Joel 3:18; Isa 25:6–8.

[14] See Mt 8:11; 22:1–14; Lk 14:12–24.

[15] See Acts 18:25–26; 19:23; 22:4; 24:14.

[16] See John Donahue, "*What Does the Lord Require? A Bibliographical Essay on the Bible and Social Justice*," rev. ed. (St. Louis: Institute of Jesuit Sources, 2000), 59.

[17] Rom 4:18–30; 8:28; Jer 29:11. See Brueggemann, *The Land*, 43.

[18] See Senior, "Beloved Aliens and Exiles," 28; Heb 11:12–15; cf. Rom 15:7.

[19] Senior, "Beloved Aliens and Exiles," 23.

[20] Mt 25:35; cf. Jn 20:11ff.; 21:1–14.

[21] Pope Francis, "Message of His Holiness Pope Francis for the 104th World Day of Migrants and Refugees," January 14, 2018.

[22] Augustine, *Quaestiones Evangeliorum*, 2:19, in Jacques-Paul Migne, *Patrologiae Cursus Completus*, Series Latina (Paris: 1844–1849), 35: 1340. Cf. *De Natura et Gratia*, chap. 50 (43), in ibid., 44: 247–90.

13

Ethics of
Social Reconciliation

The right of migrants and refugees to have rights, to belong
to a moral community, raises the further question of social
reconciliation.[1] The first right of a refugee, after all, is not to
become one. How, in a world so divided by violence, marred
by ethnic cleansing and displacement, can we restore the
biblical promise of peace? "He came and proclaimed peace to
you who were far off and peace to those who were near" (Eph
2:17)? Church teaching tells us that "peace is not merely the
absence of war, [but] an enterprise of justice."[2] Peacemaking
is grounded "solidly in the biblical vision of the kingdom of
God."[3] As scripture scholar John Donahue observes, the "biblical term for peace, *shalom*, implies wholeness, completeness,
or health. For this reason, in certain important biblical texts,
especially those describing the effect of the just use of royal
power, or in eschatological expectations of a restored kingdom, peace and justice are closely linked."[4]

Archbishop Desmond Tutu speaks in a similar vein, con-
trasting notions of retributive punishment with *Ubuntu*:

Retributive justice—in which an impersonal state hands down punishment with little consideration for victims and hardly any for the perpetrator—is not the only form of justice. I contend that there is another kind of justice, restorative justice, which was characteristic of traditional African jurisprudence. Here the central concern is not retribution or punishment but, in the spirit of *ubuntu*, the healing of breaches, the redressing of imbalances, the restoration of broken relationships.[5]

For CST, too, "righteousness [justice] and peace will kiss each other" (Ps 85:10).[6] Since the first modern encyclical, *Rerum novarum*, CST has sought "the healing of breaches." Yet the church offers no simple blueprint. Globalization, the rise of intrastate ethnic conflict, environmental degradation, and massive displacement raise new questions. We must ask how the gospel of peace can be fulfilled in *our* hearing (Lk 4:21; Eph 6:15).

As in our discussion of forced displacement, CST again poses three related questions to guide us in our "ministry of reconciliation" (2 Cor 5:18): (1) Who are the most vulnerable in our midst, for example, victims of systemic violence, bias, or exclusion? (2) What are the best means of *general redress,* that is, of securing the basic rights of those suffering ethnic cleansing, genocide, forced displacement, and so on? And (3) What are the best means of *specific redress,* that is, of securing the special rights of victims in restoring broken relationships? How we answer these questions—politically, ethically, and

religiously—will determine, in part, the role of reconciliation today.

Our first question reminds us that genuine *re*-conciliation
can never be less than just. Reconciliation presumes a common understanding of the breach or imbalance. We must, that
is, have agreed-upon conceptions of atrocity, genocide, ethnic
cleansing, and so on. Reconciliation can hardly proceed if social memory remains sharply divided—if genocide is denied,
for example, or rape or atrocity is redefined. To be sure, we
will seldom agree all the way down. Collective memory is
complex, storied, and bound to particular communitarian
traditions. Yet the "grammar" of basic human rights lets us
tell our particular stories as testimony, so that our differing
narratives bear a family resemblance. We can name the breach,
identify the broken relationship, and hear the cry of the poor,
so that rights become a grammar of dissent against atrocity.[7]

In answering the second question, we recognize that denouncing social sin is only the first step of solidarity with victims; we must also tell stories that unite. Victims' testimonies,
as in the South African Truth and Reconciliation Commission,
become a "place" for new stories to be told. Reconciliation
must redress the complex genealogy of violation, culminating
in atrocity, genocide, and so on. If the gospel of peace is to be
heard, we must "release those bound unjustly," for example, by
supremacist narratives, and "untie the thongs of the yoke" by
dismantling structures of sin, for example, the legal heritage
of gender discrimination, apartheid, or white supremacy.
Yet just as denunciation does not presume a single, grand

narrative, so telling new stories depends upon incorporating the grammar of rights in our distinctive cultures and political histories, such as the jurisprudential tradition of *Ubuntu*. And here, too, our political narratives will bear a family resemblance in embracing a fundamental responsibility for victims. Victims of systemic rights violations must be restored to their rightful place in community; the injustice of their suffering must be acknowledged and their basic human rights, including their rights to civic participation, institutionally guaranteed.

Finally, to answer the third question, we must provide fitting specific redress for the victims, for though suffering may be legion, victims are always ineluctably particular. Who has suffered, and at whose hands? Who played the role of bystander, innocent or guilty? What measure of restitution, reparation, or retribution is fitting? For to speak of social reconciliation, for example, through a general amnesty, while effacing the victim, or while abetting further victimization, is to fall prey to the hubris Jeremiah decried: "saying, 'Peace, peace,' when there is no peace" (Jer 6:14).

The rhetoric of basic human rights in our particular political narratives lets us name victim and perpetrator, while essentializing neither. Victims cannot become executioners; the rule of rights governs all. The general human rights and correlative duties implied in systemic redress are thus particularized in specific redress: victims acquire derivative rights of reparation and restitution; perpetrators have duties of repair or retribution, less for the sake of punishment than of restoring victim and perpetrator alike to moral community. Such institutional guarantees of both general and specific redress, moreover, pertain no less to the integration of refugees or forced migrants into host communities. As we noted in Chapter 11, burdens of integration should be shared equitably, so that benefits, both short term and long term, accrue to all.

Our answers to these three questions are distinct, yet never separate. Establishing or reestablishing the general rule of law in transitional justice can never efface victims. Collective memory cannot rest in cheap forgetting; political reconciliation will always, in some sense, bear the "mark of Cain" (the memory of blood that was shed). Each of our answers, moreover (recognition of atrocity, redemption of basic rights, and redress of victims) finds expression in differing registers: legal-political, ethical, and religious. Rights must be recognized in positive domestic and international law, yet both systemic and interpersonal legal redress will invariably fall short of the ethical ideal. The ethical demands of authentic reconciliation thus remain as a regulative ideal: in the wake of transitional justice, we must be vigilant, making good the cry "never again," again and again.

Vigilance also applies to the church itself. For the church, charged with the ministry of reconciliation, must itself be reconciled. As the sexual-abuse crisis attests, priests and prelates not only failed to take the victims' side, but were complicit in their victimization. The systemic distortions of clericalism masked "the abuse of power and of conscience," which, says Pope Francis, "was long ignored, kept quiet or silenced. . . . We showed no care for the little ones; we abandoned them."[8] Just as white privilege engenders an economy of exclusion, so clerical privilege, in Pope Francis's words, "leads to an excision in the ecclesial body that supports and helps to perpetuate many of the evils that we are condemning today,"[9] that is, victimization of the most vulnerable, the pursuit of power and the perquisites of office, and the scandal of denying the scandal.

Like white privilege, clericalism reflects not only personal but systemic bias—bias so deeply ingrained in institutional culture that we often fail to recognize it. Genuine reconciliation, then, requires that we name the crisis aright: not an abuse of sexuality (sins against clerical purity), but the sexual abuse of children (the gravest injustice). Redress must be not only personal but general and systemic. Structures abetting clerical privilege and episcopal malfeasance must be dismantled, and the wisdom of the laity and families fully recognized in church governance. So, too, specific redress of victims demands more than monetary compensation. Genuine reparation likewise requires unequivocal apology, repentance, and healing. "First be reconciled," Jesus says (Mt 5:24). In humility, as Pope Francis bids us, we must take the victims' side because it is our own. Prophecy begins at home, with repentance.

Questions for Reflection

1. How does reconciliation figure in the lives of those whom you accompany or serve? What does it mean for them? What traditional sources and practices of reconciliation do they have recourse to?

2. In some accounts reconciliation implies a denial of justice in the name of social harmony. Can genuine reconcili-

ation be based on forgetting past atrocities or suffering? How would those whom you accompany or serve respond?

3.   Philosopher George Santayana observed that "those who cannot remember the past are condemned to repeat it."[10] However, another political philosopher, Arthur M. Schlesinger Jr., posits, "Santayana's aphorism must be reversed: too often it is those who *can* remember the past who are condemned to repeat it."[11] How can we remember *morally* so that victims do not become executioners in an endless cycle of vengeance and recrimination?

Notes

[1] See the *Compendium of the Social Doctrine of the Church*, 196, 491–93, 517–21.

[2] Vatican II, *Gaudium et spes,* no. 78.

[3] United States Conference of Catholic Bishops, "The Challenge of Peace" (Washington, DC: USCCB, 1983), no. 25.

[4] John Donahue, *What Does the Lord Require?: A Bibliographical Essay on the Bible and Social Justice,* rev. ed. (St. Louis: Institute of Jesuit Sources, 2000), 70–71. Such biblical texts include, for example, "The effect of righteousness will be peace, / and the result of righteousness, quietness and trust forever" (Isa 32:17); and "Steadfast love and faithfulness will meet; / righteousness and peace will kiss each other" (Ps 85:10).

[5] Desmond M. Tutu, *No Future without Forgiveness* (London: Rider, 1999), 51.

[6] Similar sentiments are expressed in CST. For example, "Restorative justice . . . reflects our values and tradition. Our faith calls us to hold people accountable, to forgive, and to heal" (United States Conference of Catholic Bishops, "Responsibility, Rehabilitation, and Restoration: A Catholic Perspective on Crime and Criminal Justice" (Washington, DC: USCCB, 2000), 11.

[7] See the *Compendium of the Social Doctrine of the Church,* nos. 517–18.

[8] Pope Francis, "Letter of the Holy Father Francis to the People of God," August 20, 2018.

⁹ Ibid.

¹⁰ George Santayana, *Reason in Common Sense,* vol. 1, *The Life of Reason* (London: Constable, 1906), 284.

¹¹ Arthur M. Schlesinger Jr., *The Bitter Heritage: Vietnam and American Democracy 1941–1966* (Boston: Houghton Mifflin, 1966), 91.

14

The Role of Religion
in Social Reconciliation

Let the words of Pope Paul VI resound:

> No more one against the other, no more, never! . . .
> war never again, never again war! . . . Forgiveness,
> dialogue, reconciliation—these are the words of peace,
> in beloved Syria, in the Middle East, in all the world!
> Let us pray for reconciliation and peace, let us work for
> reconciliation and peace, and let us all become, in every
> place, men and women of reconciliation and peace![1]

In Chapter 13 we argued that genuine social reconciliation
presumes a common recognition of rights violations such
as naming atrocity, systemic redress of such violations, and
specific redress of victims' rights, for example, the right
to reparation. As seen in Figure 14.1, each of these three
elements of reconciliation plays out in differing registers;
legal-political redress, both general and specific, invariably
falls short of the *ethical* ideal. The South African Truth and

Reconciliation Commission, for instance, emerged as a political compromise, and was limited in both scope and duration. Not all legitimate claims were adjudicated, and social inequities were imperfectly redressed. Reparation was limited, yet even more extensive compensation could never pay the price of pain.[2] And religion, too, had a voice. Although the commission's writ extended only to conditional, political amnesty, talk of forgiveness figured prominently in the victim-centered hearings. According to Desmond Tutu, future reconciliation depended upon it.[3]

What role, then, should religion play in social reconciliation; and in particular, what role should religious appeals to forgiveness play in the wake of mass atrocity? How, indeed, in the face of such tragedy, is one to speak of godly things?[4] The church must walk humbly here, for our martyrs' heroism does not absolve us from complicity with the martyr makers, for example, in Rwanda or in abetting the systemic distortions of apartheid.[5] And yet, reconciliation remains a form of "prophetism" and hence of "revelation."[6]

The psalms of lament, for instance, give voice to the morally tragic character of suffering. Evil is recognized:

> O Lord, how long shall the wicked,
>   how long shall the wicked exult? . . .
> They crush your people, O Lord
>   and afflict your heritage. (Ps 94:3, 5)

But goodness (systemic redress) is also remembered—one might even say eschatologically remembered:

Elements of Reconcilia-tion →	Question 1: Critical Recognition:	Question 2: Systemic Redress:	Question 3: Specific Redress:
Interpreta-tive Regis-ters ↓	Whose basic rights are un-equally threat-ened or denied?	What are the best means of securing basic rights?	What are the best means of securing spe-cial rights?
Legal / Juridi-cal Discourse	Discovery process: victims' testi-mony, e.g., in international and local tri-bunals, truth commissions, tribunals, reporting of NGOs, etc.	Incremental real-ization of a basic rights regime: implementing or protecting, a constitutional order, impartial judiciary, etc.	Redeeming de-rivative rights: in-ternational and local tribunals, selective prosecution, provi-sion of conditional amnesty, reparation, restitution, etc.
Ethical Discourse	Integral and comprehen-sive recogni-tion of basic human rights claims and correlative duties.	Securing basic human rights claims through duties of forbear-ance, systemic protection, and provision.	Securing special rights claims through duties of redress, reparation, restitu-tion, etc.
Religious (Christian) Discourse	Lament as recognition of unjust suffer-ing: biblical ideals of jus-tice and peace fulfilled "in our hearing."	Lament as res-toration of com-munity: taking victims' side as one's own.	Lament as vindica-tion of victims. judg-ment, forgiveness, and reparation.

Figure 14.1. A Framework of Social Reconciliation

> Happy are those whom you discipline, O
>   Lord,
>   and whom you teach out of your law.
>
>   . . .
>
> For the Lord will not forsake his people;
>   he will not abandon his heritage;
> for justice will return to the righteous,
>   and all the upright in heart will fol-
>   low it. (Ps 94:12, 14–15)[7]

The lament invokes narrative, and thus, implicitly, the restoration of community and vindication of victims. The victims' cries become God's cry. Interpreted thus, the lament psalms encode the threefold elements of reconciliation: recognition, systemic address, and specific redress. And it is in this context that we may understand the place of forgiveness.

Forgiveness in the distinctively *religious* register presumes the *ethical* demands of justice.[8] In Pope Francis's words, "Forgiveness is in no way opposed to justice. It is rather the fullness of justice, leading to that tranquility of order" that involves "the deepest healing of the wounds which fester in human hearts. Justice and forgiveness are both essential to such healing."[9] Forgiveness acknowledges the victim's right to forgive, but the perpetrator has no claim to be forgiven. Authentic reconciliation presumes a primordial responsibility to the victims, that is, a recognition of the moral tragedies of genocide or apartheid, and systemic provision against their recurrence. Yet while neither ceding nor derogating their rights, victims may still, when fitting, forgo their claims (or their full satisfaction)—for Christians, in memory of Jesus, who reconciled us with God (Rom 5:10). Such forgiveness, as a form of self-sacrificial love (*agape*), transcends, even as it presupposes, the exacting rhetoric of rights. For forgiveness cannot be less than just; there is ultimately no "suspension of the ethical," to use Kierkegaard's phrase.[10]

Forgiving cannot, then, re-inscribe victimhood.[11] The mother who forgives her child's executioner acts in utter gratuity. Although morally she too must recognize the divine command upon her enemy's face—"Thou shalt not kill"—still, the dictates of morality do not entail the further command "Thou shalt love thy enemy." Here the "Thou" is utterly particular, the utterance divine. Only the mother can forgive, and her forgiveness is unexacted; the executioner has no moral claim to her forgiveness, nor can political expediency deprive the victim of what the South African jurist Albie Sachs terms her "right to forgive."[12]

Yet what is morally gratuitous may be mandated by our distinctive religious narratives—not as a *moral* duty, but rather as a response to grace. For the Christian, then, forgiveness is always a waiting on grace, and may even be the work of a lifetime. It is God's work of reconciliation in us, conforming us to the image of the crucified Christ (2 Cor 5:18–21). Remembrance of the Christian story figures in the telling of our own—that suffering is not the final word, and that our tragedy is redeemed in the tragedy of the cross. And so forgiveness may play a role not only in the end, but also at the beginning of the arduous process of political reconciliation.[13] "Because of forgiveness, there is a future," says Tutu, that is, the grace of imagining otherwise.[14]

Such imagination, as we noted in our discussion of integral ecology in chapter 5, embraces creation itself. And as Saint Paul tells us, "The whole creation has been groaning in labor pains until now" (Rom 8:22).[15] In Pope Francis's words:

> We have come to see ourselves as her [creation's] lords and masters, entitled to plunder her at will. The violence present in our hearts, wounded by sin, is also reflected in the symptoms of sickness evident in the soil, in the water, in the air and in all forms of life. This is why the earth herself, burdened and laid waste, is among the most abandoned and maltreated of our poor; she "groans in travail" (Rom 8:22) (*Laudato Si'*, 2). The environmental challenge that we are experiencing, and its human causes, affects us all (cf. *Laudato Si'*, 14) and demands our response. We can no longer remain silent before one of the greatest environmental crises in world history.[16]

Questions for Reflection

1. How is *religious* talk of reconciliation related to *political* and *ethical* demands for justice? Does faith deprive victims of their right to forgive?

2. Can forgiveness become what theologian Dietrich Bonhoeffer once called "cheap grace"?[17] Does forgiveness

imply forgetting the unjust suffering of the past? Can there be forgiveness after mass atrocity?

    3.   What political role should the churches, synagogues, mosques, and other religious institutions play in the process of transitional justice and reconciliation? Archbishop Tutu contends that there is no future without forgiveness. What *political* role does forgiveness play? Does politics wait on grace?

Notes

[1] Pope Francis, "Vigil of Prayer for Peace," 2013; see Pope Francis, *Fratelli tutti*, nos. 225–54.

  [2] Primo Levi, *The Symposium on Simon Wiesenthal, The Sunflower: On the Possibilities and Limits of Forgiveness*, rev. ed. (New York: Schocken Books, 1998), 191–92.

  [3] Desmond M. Tutu, *No Future without Forgiveness* (London: Rider, 1999), 230.

  [4] The *Compendium of the Social Doctrine of the Church* illumines several prerequisites of social reconciliation, that is, "mutual forgiveness," "justice," and ascertaining "truth about crimes perpetrated during armed conflicts" (nos. 517–18; cf. no. 196), yet says little of their precise relationship, for example, in a theology of forgiveness after mass atrocity. The interpretation offered here draws upon the resources of CST sketched in Chapter 6, but it is hardly definitive.

  [5] See J. J. Carney, *Rwanda before the Genocide: Catholic Politics and Ethnic Discourse in the Late Colonial Era* (Oxford: Oxford University Press, 2014).

  [6] Emmanuel Levinas, *Ethics and Infinity,* trans. Richard A. Cohen (Pittsburgh, PA: Duquesne University Press, 1985), 113. For Levinas, "the Infinite comes in the signifyingness of the face. The face signifies the Infinite" (105).

  [7] John Endres observes that the "language of lament bespeaks a bond, a personal relationship between the one who prays and the God of the covenant. Such language rests on faith, relies on memories—both personal and communal—of a God hearing the cry of the oppressed, of the lamenter, of the lowly . . . and God answering that cry" (John Endres, "Cry Out to

God in Our Need: Psalms of Lament," *The Way Supplement* 87 [Autumn 1996]: 41). See also Walter Brueggemann, "From Hurt to Joy, From Death to Life," *Interpretation* 28 (1974): 3–19; Claus Westermann, "The Role of the Lament in the Theology of the Old Testament," *Interpretation* 28 (1974): 20–38; Walter Brueggemann, "The Formfulness of Grief," *Interpretation* 31 (1977): 263–75; and Emmanuel Katongole, *Born from Lament: The Theology and Politics of Hope in Africa* (Grand Rapids, MI: Eerdmans, 2017).

[8] See the *Compendium of the Social Doctrine of the Church,* no. 196.

[9] Pope Francis, "Address to the Members of the Diplomatic Corps," January 9, 2017.

[10] Søren Kierkegaard, *Fear and Trembling*, trans. Sylvia Walsh (Cambridge: Cambridge University Press, 2006), 46–58.

[11] One may forgive yet still seek reparation—not as a form of punishment, but as a means of restoring broken relationships.

[12] Albie Sachs, "Reparations—Political and Psychological Considerations," *Psychoanalytic Psychotherapy in South Africa* 16, no. 25 (Summer 1993): 2.

[13] Hannah Arendt writes that forgiving "is the only reaction which does not merely re-act but acts anew and unexpectedly, unconditioned by the act which provoked it and therefore freeing from its consequences both the one who forgives and the one who is forgiven" (*The Human Condition* [Chicago: Chicago University Press, 1958], 241).

[14] In Tutu's words, "God wants to show that there is life after conflict and repression—that because of forgiveness, there is a future" (Tutu, *No Future without Forgiveness*, 230).

[15] See *Compendium of the Social Doctrine of the Church,* no. 454.

[16] Pope Francis, "Homily at Holy Mass with Representatives of the Indigenous Communities of Chiapas," February 15, 2016.

[17] Dietrich Bonhoeffer, "Costly Grace," in *The Cost of Discipleship* (Macmillan, 1948, 1976), chap. 1. Bonhoeffer writes: "Cheap grace is the preaching of forgiveness without requiring repentance, baptism without church discipline, Communion without confession, absolution without personal confession. Cheap grace is grace without discipleship, grace without the cross, grace without Jesus Christ, living and incarnate" (47).

Conclusion

Living the Gospel

As we have seen in our brief reflections, modern CST is our "moral squint"—our way of discerning the signs of the times. Where the liberal political tradition privileges a thin conception of individual dignity, and the rival communitarian tradition appeals to a thick notion of solidarity, CST invites us to imagine otherwise. Personal *dignity* binds us in *solidarity,* so that we "see" our social world, not divided into citizens and aliens, or members and strangers, but united by bonds of *near and distant neighbors.* Deriving from dignity-in-solidarity, *basic human rights* impose *duties* not only of forbearance (noninterference), but of performance (protection and provision). The political *common good* of modern, pluralist societies will thus be realized when basic human rights are structurally guaranteed in national and global regimes of *distributive* and *social justice*—regimes that preserve and protect the rights of all, including forced migrants.

As we move toward implementing policies, programs, and legal regimes, *subsidiarity* safeguards the *participatory rights* (positive liberties) of families, intermediate associations, NGOs, and supranational organizations. In making a *preferential option for the poor* (those who are systemically vulnerable), we take the victims' side in our struggle. Whose equal dignity and rights, we must ask, are unequally threatened or denied by *social sin* or systemic deprivation? Who is missing from the table of deliberation? How are rights of both general and specific redress best secured? "Passing over" to the side of the poor becomes the touchstone of legitimacy, so that citizenship binds us in solidarity with the human community present in each, especially those consigned to the margins. The *desaparecidos* (disappeared) must appear, the voiceless speak.

Linking the cry of the poor and the cry of the earth, CST is thus "small-c catholic" in appealing to an *integral humanism* and *integral ecology*. Our faith in dignity and human rights need not be explicitly religious. And yet, we have seen, there is a religious "more." For "capital-C Catholics" and Christian disciples, the dignity of labor reflects our share in divine creation, underwriting the universal destination of all created goods. So too, the stories of victims of *poverty, racism, forced migration*, or *ethnic cleansing* often recall *their* hope against hope in the liberating love of God. Accompaniment reflects a spirituality of biblical hospitality: not the pity of the powerful, but compassion (suffering with). The disciple must take the victim's side as his or her own, must become a neighbor. For the neighbor is "not the one I encounter in my journey but the one in whose journey I place myself."[1] It is a journey shared when hosts become guests and guests become hosts.

And it is a perilous journey, marked by lament, as we walk in the way of *shalom* (Lk 1:79). In seeking *reconciliation* with neighbors "far and near" (Eph 2:17), as Teilhard de Chardin once said, "we must trust in the *slow* work of God"[2] inspiring us to live into grace and blessing, to forgive as we are forgiven. Finally, to place ourselves with the crucified people is to be placed with the crucified One. For the great theologian Karl Rahner, this was our implied *faith*. And, as Matthew's parable of the last judgment reminds us, it may be lived even when explicit belief is lacking (Mt 25:37–40). One need not be explicitly Catholic or Christian to share this fundamental *hope* in the risk or wager of a life we call *love*.[3] That is enough, and it is everything.

A final word as we look to the future. CST, as part of a living faith, will continue to develop as the church draws on scriptural, theological, and spiritual wisdom. New forms of knowledge, such as artificial intelligence, genetics, and cosmology, will give rise to new wisdom and novel reappropriations of tradition as the gospel is proclaimed today, in our hearing (Lk 4:21). Wisdom is thus handed on (*traditio*) as we ourselves become ancestors. Looking not only to the methodological implications of such development, but to its sources in the "sense of the faithful," the teaching church will be challenged to integrate spiritual traditions with social and sexual doctrine.

Prophetic humility demands that we acknowledge where we have strayed from the way, sometimes gravely so, as in the sexual abuse crisis. Prophecy is never extinguished, but only a truly repentant church can be prophetic. A living tradition will seek the word of the crucified One in a crucified people, those whom history still consigns to the margins. Women's voices must be fully incorporated into the body of CST—not only in its reception, but in its ongoing interpretation. The option for the historically excluded must be applied to the *teaching* itself. As Pope Francis has so eloquently reminded us in *Laudato Si'* and *Fratelli tutti*, the encyclical tradition is not an end, but a beginning.

The tradition unfolds, then, not as an extended set of inferences contained in a rulebook, but as a tapestry, woven and rewoven anew in each generation. Dialogue, so dear to Pope Francis, plays out over time in what African theologians call palaver—words in a communitarian reconciliation process. Doctrine thus remains vital, attesting a multiplicity of influences not only of differing cultures (inculturation), but of differing denominational and faith traditions. For finally, the threads are woven in a pattern we do not know, and by a hand we do not see—and so we press on, hoping against hope for that day when we will see what the Weaver always intended. And as always, our flawed and stubborn words must end in praise.

We began this guide with Pope Francis's "Prayer for Our Earth,"[4] offered for all who entertain belief in a loving God. We end with the companion prayer for Christians entitled "A Christian Prayer in Union with Creation." These two prayers conclude the encyclical *Laudato Si'*:

> Father, we praise you with all your crea-
> tures.
> They came forth from your all-powerful
> hand;

they are yours, filled with your presence
      and your tender love.
Praise be to you!

Son of God, Jesus,
through you all things were made.
You were formed in the womb of Mary
      our Mother,
you became part of this earth,
and you gazed upon this world with hu-
      man eyes.
Today you are alive in every creature
in your risen glory.
Praise be to you!

Holy Spirit, by your light
you guide this world towards the Father's
      love
and accompany creation as it groans in
      travail.
You also dwell in our hearts
and you inspire us to do what is good.
Praise be to you!

Triune Lord, wondrous community of
      infinite love,
teach us to contemplate you
in the beauty of the universe,

for all things speak of you.
Awaken our praise and thankfulness
for every being that you have made.
Give us the grace to feel profoundly
        joined
to everything that is.

God of love, show us our place in this
        world
as channels of your love
for all the creatures of this earth,
for not one of them is forgotten in your
        sight.
Enlighten those who possess power and
        money
that they may avoid the sin of indiffer-
        ence,
that they may love the common good,
        advance the weak,
and care for this world in which we live.
The poor and the earth are crying out.
O Lord, seize us with your power and
        light,
help us to protect all life,
to prepare for a better future,
for the coming of your Kingdom
of justice, peace, love and beauty.
Praise be to you!
Amen.[5]

Notes

[1] Gustavo Gutiérrez, "Toward a Theology of Liberation," trans. Alfred T. Hennelly, in *Liberation Theology: A Documentary History*, ed. Alfred T. Hennelly, 62–76 (Maryknoll, NY: Orbis Books, 1990), 74.

[2] Pierre Teihard de Chardin, SJ, *The Making of Mind: Letters of a Soldier-Priest 1914–19*, trans René Hague (New York: Harper and Row, 1965), 57 (emphasis in original).

[3] As noted in Chapter 6, duties and virtues of discipleship (presuming, but transcending our "common faith" in dignity and rights) are distinctively but not uniquely Christian. Believers of other faiths or of no faith may "cross over" to the world of the poor. And, like the Samaritan of Luke's Gospel, they may teach Christians the meaning of the law.

[4] Pope Francis, *Laudato Si',* no. 246.

[5] Ibid.

Appendix

A Word about Intrinsic Evil

CST, we argued, is less a set of abstract, disembodied rules than a wisdom and way of life, demanding discernment. But, some may object, what about specific rules forbidding "intrinsically evil" actions? Such rules seem to bind unconditionally, apart from circumstances or intentions. In *Splendor Veritatis*, for example, Pope John Paul II states: "Without in the least denying the influence on morality exercised by circumstances and especially by intentions, the Church teaches that 'there exist acts which *per se* and in themselves, independently of circumstances, are always seriously wrong by reason of their object.'"[1] In appealing to Catholic voters, for example, the US bishops contend that "the moral obligation to oppose policies promoting intrinsically evil acts has a special claim on our consciences and our actions."[2] Some bishops assert that opposing policies promoting intrinsically evil acts is nonnegotiable. Laws permitting intrinsic evil, they say, are themselves intrinsically evil, so voting for them (or even for someone supporting them) entails cooperation in evil.

To say an act is intrinsically evil is simply to say that, by its very nature, it is morally impermissible—no further appeal to intentions or circumstances can justify it. But to name an act intrinsically evil tells us little of its comparative moral gravity. Saint Augustine, for instance, believed that lying was always impermissible, but we would claim that not all lies are equally grave. Nor are all equally grave acts intrinsically evil. Endemic poverty, famine, and neglect of our common home are gravely wrong, even if they do not fall under the rubrics of intrinsic evil.

Appealing to modern CST on human rights, Pope John Paul II quotes the Second Vatican Council in giving examples of acts that are always seriously wrong:

> Whatever is hostile to life itself, such as any kind of homicide, genocide, abortion, euthanasia and voluntary suicide; whatever violates the integrity of the human person, such as mutilation, physical and mental torture and attempts to coerce the spirit; whatever is offensive to human dignity, such as subhuman living conditions, arbitrary imprisonment, deportation, slavery, prostitution and trafficking in women and children; degrading conditions of work which treat labourers as mere instruments of profit, and not as free responsible persons.[3]

Such practices, says Pope John Paul II, are intrinsically evil, having a special claim on our consciences. Indeed, as we saw in our discussion of the option for the poor in Chapter 5, the gravity of abortion rests precisely in the threat it poses to the most vulnerable in our midst.

Finally, naming an act intrinsically evil does not dictate a simple legislative remedy. Personal choice (that *I* cannot promote intrinsically evil acts) cannot be writ large on the body politic of a religiously pluralist democracy. As Thomas Aquinas realized, not all wrongful acts or practices are fit subjects of legislative proscription. Pope John Paul II addresses the case of legislators and abortion laws:

> A particular problem of conscience can arise in cases where a legislative vote would be decisive for the passage of a more restrictive law, aimed at limiting the number of authorized abortions, in place of a more permissive law already passed or ready to be voted on. . . . In a case like the one just mentioned, when it is not possible to overturn or completely abrogate a pro-abortion law, an elected official, whose absolute personal opposition to procured abortion was well known, could licitly support proposals aimed at limiting the harm done by such a law and at lessening its negative consequences at the level of general opinion and public morality. This does not in fact represent an illicit cooperation with an unjust law, but rather a legitimate and proper attempt to limit its evil aspects. [4]

Clearly, legislators must ask what politically feasible law or juridical decision will best protect the rights of the most vulnerable. And this is an exercise of *prudence*.

After discussing that special case, Pope John Paul II returns to the more general situation, emphasizing that

Christians, like all people of good will, are called upon under grave obligation of conscience not to cooperate formally in practices which, even if permitted by civil legislation, are contrary to God's law. Indeed, from the moral standpoint, it is never licit to cooperate formally in evil.[5]

In conclusion, then, the label *intrinsic evil* does *not* determine the comparative moral gravity of abortion or poverty, much less of other intrinsically evil actions, such as trafficking of women and children. Prudence has a role in discerning how best to protect the basic rights of the most vulnerable. For Aquinas, *all* morality is prudential (in the Aristotelian sense of practical reason ordered to the common good). Indeed, it is prudence that tells us certain acts or practices are impermissible, such as systemic racism or the modern slavery of human trafficking; and it is prudence that determines which laws or juridical decisions best promote the common good.[6]

Notes

[1] John Paul II, *Splendor Veritatis*, no. 80.

[2] United States Conference of Catholic Bishops, "Forming Consciences for Faithful Citizenship: A Call to Political Responsibility from the Catholic Bishops of the United States with Introductory Note" (November 2015), no. 37.

[3] Second Vatican Council, *Gaudium et spes*, no. 27.

[4] Pope John Paul II, *Evangelium vitae*, no. 73.

[5] Ibid., no. 74.

[6] The US bishops include racism among acts or practices that are intrinsically evil. See "Forming Consciences for Faithful Citizenship," no. 23.

References

Catholic Social Teaching: The Documentary Heritage

All conciliar texts, encyclicals, apostolic exhortations, apostolic letters, homilies, and addresses can be found at www.vatican.va. The principal texts are listed below.

Pope Leo XIII, *Rerum novarum* (On the Condition of Labor), 1891.

Pope Pius XI, *Quadragesimo anno* (After Forty Years), 1931.

Pope John XXIII, *Mater et magistra* (Christianity and Social Progress), 1961.

———. *Pacem in terris* (Peace on Earth), 1963.

Second Vatican Council, *Gaudium et spes* (Pastoral Constitution on the Church in the Modern World), 1965.

———. *Dignitatis humanae* (Declaration on Religious Freedom), 1965.

Pope Paul VI, *Populorum progressio* (On the Development of Peoples), 1967.

———. *Octogesima adveniens* (A Call to Action), 1971.

———. *Evangelii nuntiandi* (Evangelization in the Modern World), 1975.

Pope John Paul II, *Laborem exercens* (On Human Work), 1981.

———. *Sollicitudo rei socialis* (On Social Concern), 1987.

———. *Centesimus annus* (The Hundredth Year), 1991.

———. *Veritatis splendor* (The Splendor of Truth), 1993.

———. *Evangelium vitae* (The Gospel of Life), 1995.

Pontifical Council for Justice and Peace, *Compendium of the Social Doctrine of the Church,* 2004.

Pope Benedict XVI, *Deus caritas est* (God Is Love), 2005.

———. *Caritas in veritate* (Charity in Truth), 2009.

Pope Francis, *Evangelii gaudium* (The Joy of the Gospel), 2013.

————. *Laudato Si'* (On Care for Our Common Home), 2015.
————. *Fratelli tutti* (On Fraternity and Social Friendship), 2020.

For texts of the synods of bishops, see
www.vatican.va.roman_curia/synod/index.htm.

For an English translation of the 1971 Synod of Bishops document *Justitia in mundo* (Justice in the World), 1971, see David J. O'Brien and Thomas A. Shannon, eds. *Catholic Social Thought: Encyclicals and Documents from Pope Leo XIII to Pope Francis.* Third revised edition. Maryknoll, NY: Orbis Books, 2016.

For papal teachings and analyses of social issues, see *Dicastery for Promoting Integral Human Development*. (On January 1, 2017, the dicastery was formed by the merger of the Pontifical Council for Justice and Peace, the Pontifical Council *Cor Unum*, the Pontifical Council for the Pastoral Care of Migrants and Itinerant People, and the Pontifical Council for Health Care Workers. A section of the dicastery, under the guidance of Pope Francis, deals specifically with issues concerning migrants, refugees, and victims of human trafficking. *Caritas Internationalis* likewise falls under the dicastery.)
http://www.humandevelopment.va/en/il-dicastero.html.

United States Conference of Catholic Bishops documents can be found at the USCCB website: www.usccb.org. (Other pastoral letters of episcopal conferences may be found at their respective websites.)

The Challenge of Peace, 1983.

Economic Justice for All, 1986.

The Harvest of Justice Is Sown in Peace, 1993.

A Decade after Economic Justice for All, 1995.

Strangers No Longer (joint statement from the bishops of the United States and Mexico), 2003.

Select Bibliography

Alexander, Michelle. *The New Jim Crow: Mass Incarceration in the Age of Colorblindness.* Revised edition. New York: The New Press, 2012.

Ambrose. "On the Duties of the Clergy." Translated by H. De Romestin, with the assistance of E. De Romestin and H. T. F. Duckworth. New York: Christian Literature Publishing, 1886.

Aquinas, Thomas. *Summa Theologiae*. Second revised edition. Translated by Fathers of the English Dominican Province. New York: Benziger Bros., 1948.

Arendt, Hannah. "The Perplexities of the Rights of Man." In *The Origins of Totalitarianism*. New York: Harcourt, Brace and World, 1966.

Augustine. *Quaestiones Evangeliorum*, 2:19. In Jacques-Paul Migne, *Patrologiae Cursus Completus*, Series Latina. Paris: 1844–1849, 35:1340.

———. "Reply to Faustus the Manichaean." Translated by Richard Stothert. Buffalo, NY: Christian Publishing, 1886.

———. "Letter to Marcellinus," 138. Translated by J. G. Cunningham. In *Nicene and Post-Nicene Fathers, First Series*, volume 1, edited by Philip Schaff. Buffalo, NY: Christian Literature Publishing, 1887.

———. *De Natura et Gratia*. In Jacques-Paul Migne, *Patrologiae Cursus Completus*. Series Latina. 1844–1849, 44:247–90.

———. "Commentary on Psalm 125." In *Expositions on the Books of Psalms*, volume 5, translated by H. M. Wilkins. Volume 37 of *A Library of the Fathers of the Holy Catholic Church*. London: F. and J. Rivington, 1835, 543.

———. Letter 189, "Letter to Boniface." Translated by J. G. Cunningham. In *Nicene and Post-Nicene Fathers, First Series*, volume 1, edited by Philip Schaff. Buffalo, NY: Christian Literature Publishing Co., 1887.

———. *Sermo Dom*. I, xx, 63 and 70; Epist. 138, ii, 14. In *Retractationes* I, xix, 1. Cited in Roland Bainton, *Christian Attitudes toward War and Peace: A Historical Survey and Critical Re-evaluation*. Nashville, TN: Abingdon, 1960.

Bainton, Roland. *Christian Attitudes toward War and Peace: A Historical Survey and Critical Re-evaluation*. Nashville, TN: Abingdon, 1960.

Benhabib, Seyla. *The Rights of Others: Aliens, Residents, and Citizens*. Cambridge: Cambridge University Press, 2004.

Bernardin, Joseph Cardinal. "The Consistent Ethic of Life and Public Policy." In *A Moral Vision for America*, edited by John P. Langan, SJ. Washington, DC: Georgetown University Press, 1998.

Biko, Steve. *I Write What I Like: Selected Writings*. Chicago: University of Chicago Press, 2002.

Bolt, Robert. *A Man for All Seasons*. New York: Random House, 1990.

Boyle, Gregory. *Tattoos on the Heart: The Power of Boundless Compassion*. New York: Free Press, 2010.

Brackley, Dean. *The Call to Discernment in Troubled Times: New Perspective on the Transformative Wisdom of Ignatius of Loyola.* New York: Crossroad, 2004.

Brigham, Erin M. *See, Judge, Act: Catholic Social Teaching and Service Learning.* Revised edition. Winona, MN: Anselm Academic, 2018.

Brueggemann, Walter. "From Hurt to Joy, From Death to Life." *Interpretation* 28 (1974): 3–19.

———. "The Formfulness of Grief." *Interpretation* 31 (1977): 263–75.

———. *The Land.* Second edition. Minneapolis: Fortress Press, 1977.

Bujo, Bénézet. *African Theology in Its Social Context.* Translated by John O'Donohue. Nairobi, Kenya: St. Paul, 1986.

Cahill, Lisa Sowle. *Global Justice, Christology, and Christian Ethics*, New Studies in Christian Ethics, edited by Robin Gill. New York: Cambridge University Press, 2013.

———. *Blessed Are the Peacemakers: Pacifism, Just War, and Peacebuilding.* Minneapolis: Fortress Press, 2019.

Camus, Albert. *The Plague.* Translated by Stuart Gilbert. New York: Alfred A. Knopf, 1960.

Carney, J. J. *Rwanda before the Genocide: Catholic Politics and Ethnic Discourse in the Late Colonial Era.* Oxford: Oxford University Press, 2014.

Coates, Ta-Nehisi. "The Black Family in the Age of Mass Incarceration." *The Atlantic.* October, 2015.

Collier, Elizabeth W., and Charles R. Strain, eds. *Religious and Ethical Perspectives on Global Migration.* Lanham, MD: Lexington Books, 2014.

Copeland, M. Shawn. *Enfleshing Freedom: Body, Race, and Being.* Minneapolis: Fortress Press, 2010.

Curran, Charles. *Catholic Social Teaching 1891–Present: A Historical, Theological, and Ethical Analysis.* Washington, DC: Georgetown University Press, 2002.

———. "The Reception of Catholic Social and Economic Teaching in the United States." In *Modern Catholic Social Teaching: Commentaries and Interpretations,* edited by Kenneth R. Himes, 469–92. Washington, DC: Georgetown University Press, 2004.

Dalai Lama, *Ethics for the New Millennium.* New York: Riverhead Books, 2001.

Day, Dorothy. *Selected Writings.* Edited by Robert Ellsberg. Maryknoll, NY: Orbis Books, 1998.

DeBerri, Edward P., James E. Hug, Peter J. Henriot, and Michael J. Schultheis. *Catholic Social Teaching: Our Best Kept Secret.* Fourth revised edition. Maryknoll, NY: Orbis Books, 2003.

d' Entrèves, Alexander Passerin. *Natural Law: An Introduction to Legal Philosophy*. New York: Routledge, 1994.

Donahue, John R. "The Bible and Catholic Social Teaching: Will This Engagement Lead to Marriage?" In *Modern Catholic Social Teaching: Commentaries and Interpretations*, edited by Kenneth R. Himes, 9–40. Washington, DC: Georgetown University Press, 2004.

———. "Biblical Perspectives on Justice." In *The Faith That Does Justice*, Woodstock Series #2, edited by J. Haughey. New York: Paulist Press, 1977.

———. *What Does the Lord Require? A Bibliographical Essay on the Bible and Social Justice*. Revised edition. St. Louis: Institute of Jesuit Sources, 2000.

———. *Seek Justice That You May Live: Reflections and Resources on the Bible and Social Justice*. Mahwah, NJ: Paulist Press, 2014.

Dostoevsky, Fyodor. *The Brothers Karamazov*. Translated by Richard Pevear and Larissa Volokhonsky. New York: Vintage Classics, 1990.

Drèze, Jean, and Amartya Sen. *Hunger and Public Action*. Oxford: Clarendon, 1989.

Dworkin, Ronald. *Taking Rights Seriously*. Cambridge, MA: Harvard University, 1978.

Éla, Jean-Marc. "Christianity and Liberation in Africa." In *Paths of African Theology*, edited by Rosino Gibellini. Maryknoll, NY: Orbis Books, 1994.

Emerson, Ralph Waldo. "The Essay on Self-Reliance." East Aurora, NY: Roycrofters, 1908.

Endres, John. "Cry Out to God in Our Need: Psalms of Lament," *The Way Supplement* 87 (Autumn 1996): 34–44.

Endres, John C., and Elizabeth Liebert. *A Retreat with the Psalms: Resources for Personal and Communal Prayer*. Mahwah, NJ: Paulist Press, 2001.

Farley, Margaret A. *Just Love: A Framework for Christian Sexual Ethics*. New York: Continuum, 2006.

Friedman, Milton. "Good Ends, Bad Means." In *The Catholic Challenge to the American Economy: Reflections on the US Bishops' Pastoral Letter on Catholic Social Teaching and the US Economy*, edited by Thomas M. Gannon, SJ. Macmillan: New York, 1987.

Gaillardetz, Richard R. "The Ecclesiological Foundations of Modern Catholic Social Teaching." In *Modern Catholic Social Teaching: Commentaries and Interpretations*, edited by Kenneth R. Himes, 72–99. Washington, DC: Georgetown University Press, 2004.

Gewirth, Alan. *Human Rights*. Chicago: University of Chicago Press, 1982.

―――. *The Community of Rights*. Chicago: University of Chicago Press, 1996.

Goodwin-Gill, Guy S., and Jane McAdam. *The Refugee in International Law*. Second edition. Oxford: Clarendon, 1966.

Grotius, Hugo. "Prologue." In *On the Law of War and Peace,* edited by Stephen C. Neff. Cambridge: Cambridge University Press, 2012.

Gutiérrez, Gustavo. *A Theology of Liberation: Fifteenth Anniversary Edition*. Translated by Sister Caridad Inda and John Eagleson. Maryknoll, NY: Orbis Books, 1988.

―――. "Toward a Theology of Liberation" (July 1968). Translated by Alfred T. Hennelly. In *Liberation Theology: A Documentary History*, edited by Alfred T. Hennelly, 62–76. Maryknoll, NY: Orbis Books, 1990.

―――. *The Truth Shall Make You Free: Confrontations*. Translated by Matthew J. O'Connell. Maryknoll, NY: Orbis Books, 1990.

―――. *We Drink from Our Own Wells*. Translated by Matthew J. O'Connell. Maryknoll, NY: Orbis Books, 2003.

Heyer, Kristin. *Kinship across Borders: A Christian Ethics of Immigration*. Washington, DC: Georgetown University Press, 2012.

Himes, Kenneth R., ed. *Modern Catholic Social Teaching: Commentaries and Interpretations*. Washington, DC: Georgetown University Press, 2004.

Hobbes, Thomas. *Leviathan*. In *British Moralists: 1650–1800,* edited by D. D. Raphael, volume 1. Oxford: Clarendon Press, 1969.

Hohfeld, Wesley. *Fundamental Legal Conceptions*. New Haven, CT: Yale Univesity Press, 1923.

Hollenbach, David. *Claims in Conflict: Retrieving and Renewing the Catholic Human Rights Tradition*. New York: Paulist Press, 1979.

―――. *The Common Good and Christian Ethics*. Cambridge: Cambridge University Press, 2002.

―――. *Humanity in Crisis: Ethical and Religious Response to Refugees*. Washington, DC: Georgetown University Press, 2019.

Hopkins, Gerard Manley. *The Poems of Gerard Manley Hopkins*. Fourth edition. W. H. Gardner and H. M. MacKenzie. New York: Oxford University Press, 1970.

Hountondji, Paulin J. "The Master's Voice: Remarks on the Problem of Human Rights in Africa." In *Philosophical Foundations of Human Rights*, introduction by Paul Ricoeur. UNESCO: Paris, 1986.

Ignatius of Loyola. *The Spiritual Exercises of Saint Ignatius.* Translated by George E. Ganss, SJ. St. Louis: Institute of Jesuit Sources, 1992.

Isasi-Díaz, Ada María. *En la Lucha / In the Struggle: A Hispanic Women's Liberation Theology.* Minneapolis: Fortress Press, 1993.

Kant, Immanuel. *The Metaphysical Elements of Justice.* Translated by John Ladd. Indianapolis: Bobbs-Merrill, 1965.

Karris, Robert J. "The Gospel according to Luke." In *The New Jerome Biblical Commentary*, edited by Raymond E. Brown, SS, Joseph A. Fitzmyer, SJ, and Roland E. Murphy, OCarm, 675–721. London: Geoffrey Chapman, 1990.

Katongole, Emmanuel. *Born from Lament: The Theology and Politics of Hope in Africa.* Grand Rapids, MI: Eerdmans, 2017.

Kierkegaard, Søren. *The Concept of Irony.* Translated by Howard V. Hong and Edna H. Hong. *Kierkegaard's Writings*, volume 2, 272–323. Princeton, NJ: Princeton University Press, 1992.

———. *Either / Or*, Part II. Translated by Howard V. Hong and Edna H. Hong. *Kierkegaard's Writings*, volume 4. Princeton, NJ: Princeton University Press, 1987.

———. *Fear and Trembling.* Translated by Sylvia Walsh. Cambridge: Cambridge University Press, 2006.

———. *Works of Love.* Translated by Howard and Edna Hong. New York: Harper and Row, 1962.

King, Martin Luther, Jr. "Letter from Birmingham City Jail." In *A Testament of Hope: The Essential Writings of Martin Luther King, Jr.*, edited by James Melvin Washington, 289–302. San Francisco: Harper and Row, 1986.

Koenig, John. "Hospitality." In *The Anchor Bible Dictionary*, volume 3, edited by David Noel Freedman, 299–301. New York: Doubleday, 1992.

Levi, Primo. *The Symposium on Simon Wiesenthal, The Sunflower: On the Possibilities and Limits of Forgiveness.* Revised edition. New York: Schocken Books, 1998.

Levinas, Emmanuel. *Ethics and Infinity.* Translated by Richard A. Cohen. Pittsburgh: Duquesne University Press, 1985.

Loescher, Gil, and James Milner. *Protracted Refugee Situations: Domestic and International Security Implications.* London: International Institute for Strategic Studies, 2005.

Lyotard, Jean-François. "The Other's Rights." In *The Politics of Human Rights*, edited by Obrad Saviæ, 181–88. London: Verso, 1999.

Magesa, Laurenti. *African Religion: The Moral Tradition of Abundant Life*. Maryknoll, NY: Orbis Books, 1997.

Maritain, Jacques. "The Person and the Common Good." In *The Social and the Political Philosophy of Jacques Maritain*, edited by Joseph W. Evans and Leo R. Ward. New York: Charles Scribner's Sons, 1955.

Martin, Susan. "Justice, Women's Rights, and Forced Migration." In *Refugee Rights, Ethics Advocacy, and Africa*, edited by David Hollenbach, SJ, 137–60. Washington, DC: Georgetown University Press, 2008.

Massaro, Thomas, SJ. *Living Justice: Catholic Social Teaching in Action*. Third classroom edition. Lanham, MD: Rowman and Littlefield, 2016.

Massingale, Bryan. *Racial Justice and the Catholic Church*. Maryknoll, NY: Orbis Books, 2010.

Mich, Marvin L. Krier. *Catholic Social Teaching and Movements*. Mystic, CT: Twenty-Third Publications, 1998.

Murray, John Courtney. *We Hold These Truths: Catholic Reflections on the American Proposition*. New York: Sheed and Ward, 1960.

———. "This Matter of Religious Freedom." *America* 112 (January 9, 1965).

———. "Memo to Cardinal Cushing concerning Contraception Legislation." In *Bridging the Sacred and the Secular: Selected Writings of John Courtney Murray, SJ*, edited by Leon Hooper, 81–86. Washington, DC: Georgetown University Press, 1994.

Mveng, Engelbert. "Black African Art as Cosmic Liturgy and Religious Language." In *African Theology en Route: Papers from the Pan-African Conference of Third World Theologians, December 17–23, 1977, Accra, Ghana*, edited by Kofi Appiah-Kobi and Sergio Torres, 137–42. Maryknoll, NY: Orbis Books, 1977.

Nowrojee, Binaifer. "Sexual Violence, Gender Roles, and Displacement." In *Refugee Rights, Ethics Advocacy, and Africa*, edited by David Hollenbach, SJ, 125–36. Washington, DC: Georgetown University Press, 2008.

Nozick, Robert. *Anarchy, State, and Utopia*. Oxford: Basil Blackwell, 1974.

Okin, Susan Moller. "Gender Inequality and Cultural Differences." In *Political Theory* 22, no. 1 (February 1994): 5–24.

O'Neill, Onora. "Justice, Capabilities, and Vulnerabilities." In *Women, Culture, and Development: A Study of Human Capabilities*, edited by Martha C.

Nussbaum and Jonathan Glover, 140–52. Oxford: Clarendon Press, 1995.

Orend, Brian. "Justice after War." *Ethics and International Affairs* 16 (2002): 43–56.

Outka, Gene. *Agape: An Ethical Analysis.* New Haven, CT: Yale University Press, 1972.

———. "Respect for Persons." In *The Westminster Dictionary of Christian Ethics,* edited by James F. Childress and John MacQuarrie, 541–45. Philadelphia: Westminster Press, 1986.

Panikkar, Raimon. *The Cosmotheandric Experience: Emerging Religious Consciousness.* Edited by Scott Eastham. Maryknoll, NY: Orbis Books, 1993.

Pelikan, Jaroslav. *The Vindication of Tradition.* New Haven, CT: Yale University Press, 1987.

Pohl, Christine D. *Making Room: Recovering Hospitality as a Christian Tradition.* Grand Rapids, MI: Eerdmans, 1999.

Rahner, Karl. "On the Question of a Formal Existential Ethics." In *Theological Investigations* 2, translated by Karl H. Kruger, 217–34. Baltimore: Helicon, 1963.

———. "Karl Rahner, The 'Commandment' of Love in Relation to the Other Commandments." In *Theological Investigations* 5, translated by Karl H. Kruger, 439–59. New York: Seabury, 1966.

———. "Reflections on the Unity of the Love of Neighbour and the Love of God." In *Theological Investigations* 6, translated by Karl and Boniface Kruger, 231–49. New York: Seabury, 1974.

———. "The Theology of Freedom." In *Theological Investigations* 6, translated by Karl and Boniface Kruger, 178–96. New York: Seabury, 1974.

Rawls, John. *A Theory of Justice.* Revised edition. Cambridge: The Belknap Press of Harvard University Press, 1999.

———. *Political Liberalism.* New York: Colombia University Press, 2005.

Richard Rorty. "The Priority of Democracy to Philosophy." In *The Virginia Statute for Religious Freedom: Its Evolution and Consequences in American History*, edited by Merrill D. Peterson and Robert C. Vaughan. New York/Cambridge: Cambridge University Press, 1988.

Romero, Archbishop Óscar. "The Political Dimension of the Faith from the Perspective of the Option for the Poor" (University of Louvain, February 2, 1980). In *Liberation Theology: A Documentary History*, edited by Alfred T. Hennelly. Maryknoll, NY: Orbis Books, 1990.

Runzo, Joseph, Nancy M. Martin, and Arvind Sharma, eds. *Human Rights and Responsibilities in the World Religions,* The Library of Global Ethics and Religion, volume 4. Oxford: Oneworld, 2002.

Sachs, Albie. "Reparations—Political and Psychological Considerations." *Psychoanalytic Psychotherapy in South Africa* 16, no. 25 (Summer 1993).

Sandel, Michael. "Introduction." In *Liberalism and Its Critics*, edited by Michael Sandel. New York: New York University Press, 1984.

Santayana, George. *Reason in Common Sense*. Volume 1, *The Life of Reason*. London: Constable, 1906.

Schlesinger, Arthur M., Jr. *The Bitter Heritage: Vietnam and American Democracy*. Boston: Houghton Mifflin, 1966.

Schrage, Wolfgang. *The Ethics of the New Testament*. Translated by David E. Green. Philadelphia: Fortress, 1988.

Schuck, Michael, "When the Shooting Stops: Missing Elements in Just War Theory." *The Christian Century* 101 (October 26, 1999): 982–84.

Sen, Amartya. *Development as Freedom*. New York: Anchor Books, 1999.

Senior, Donald. "Beloved Aliens and Exiles." In *A Promised Land, A Perilous Journey: Theological Perspectives on Migration,* edited by Daniel G. Groody and Gioacchino Campese, 20–34. Notre Dame, IN: University of Notre Dame Press, 2009.

Shue, Henry. *Basic Rights: Subsistence, Affluence, and US Foreign Policy*. Princeton, NJ: Princeton University Press, 1980.

Sobrino, Jon. *The Spirituality of Liberation: Toward Political Holiness*. Translated by Robert R. Barr. Maryknoll, NY: Orbis Books, 1988.

———. "Companions of Jesus." In Jon Sobrino, Ignacio Ellacuría et al., *Companions of Jesus: The Jesuit Martyrs of El Salvador*, 3–56. Maryknoll, NY: Orbis Books, 1990.

Stevenson, Bryan. *Just Mercy: A Story of Justice and Redemption*. New York: Spiegel and Grau, 2014.

Stuhlmueller, Carroll. "Option for the Poor: Old Testament Directives." In *Economic Justice: CTU's Pastoral Commentary on the Bishops' Letter on the Economy*, edited by John Pawlikowski and Donald Senior, 19–27. Washington, DC: Paulist Press, 1988.

Taylor, Charles. *Modern Social Imaginaries*. Edited by Dilip Parameshwar Gaonkar, Benjamin Lee, Jane Kramer, and Michael Warner. Durham, NC: Duke University Press, 2004.

Teilhard de Chardin, Pierre. *The Making of Mind: Letters of a Soldier-Priest 1914–19.* Translated by René Hague. Harper and Row: New York: 1965.

Tocqueville, Alexis de. *Democracy in America.* Volume 2, part 2. Translated by George Lawrence. Edited by J. P. Mayer. New York: HarperCollins, 1969.

Tutu, Desmond M. *Hope and Suffering: Sermons and Speeches.* Compiled by Mothobi Mutloatse. Edited by John Webster. Grand Rapids, MI: Eerdmans 1983.

———. *No Future without Forgiveness.* London: Rider, 1999.

United Nations. Universal Declaration of Human Rights. December 10, 1948.

Walzer, Michael. *Just and Unjust Wars: A Moral Argument with Historical Illustrations.* Third edition. New York: Basic Books, 1977.

———. *Exodus and Revolution.* New York: Basic Books, 1985.

Weil, Simone. "Reflections on the Right Use of School Studies with a View to the Love of God." In *Waiting for God,* translated by Emma Craufurd, 105–16. New York: G. P. Putnam's Sons, 1951.

Westermann, Claus. "The Role of the Lament in the Theology of the Old Testament." *Interpretation* 28 (1974): 20–38.

Wuthnow, Robert. *God and Mammon in America.* New York: Free Press, 1994.

Further Reading: Commentaries and Criticism

Clark, Meghan J. *The Vision of Catholic Social Thought: The Virtue of Solidarity and the Praxis of Human Rights.* Minneapolis: Fortress, 2018. An original account of the integration of human rights rhetoric and solidarity in Catholic social teaching.

Groody, Daniel G. *Globalization, Spirituality, and Justice: Navigating the Path to Peace.* Revised edition. Maryknoll, NY: Orbis Books, 2015. A compelling interpretation and application of Catholic social teaching.

O'Brien, David J., and Thomas A. Shannon, eds. *Catholic Social Thought: Encyclicals and Documents from Pope Leo XIII to Pope Francis.* Third revised edition. Maryknoll, NY: Orbis Books, 2016. A source book with brief commentaries on the principal texts.

Schlag, Martin, ed. *Handbook of Catholic Social Teaching: A Guide for Christians in the World Today.* Foreword by Peter K. A. Cardinal Turkson. Washington, DC: Catholic University of America Press, 2017. A digest of the *Compendium of Catholic Social Doctrine* in question-and-answer form.

Index